"I was very excited to go on the Make Your Own Video prog
I got used to very quickly was talking to a camera – something I'd always felt extremely uncomfortable about. I learnt so many tips and tricks from Ruth that I just wouldn't learn from someone without that amount of experience. All the learners were from very different sectors but the course was so versatile that we all took something extremely useful from it." Juliet Clare Bell, children's author

"Thank you for giving me the opportunity to make my own videos. You made it so straightforward. I worked through the handbook carefully and then by using the storyboards and instructions, was able to create my own promotional video. I was a bit worried about the editing part but once I got stuck in I found it was quite easy. I am already looking forward to making more videos and I'm confident they'll get better with practice." Caroline Nash, actor and theatre company owner

"In just two days, Make Your Own Video Academy has taken me from knowing nothing about how to set up, film and edit a video to being able to make one, which is amazing! As learners we weren't overburdened with information. The workshop was enjoyable and to the point and I realised just how effective it was when I went away and made videos on my own afterwards. I would thoroughly recommend Make Your Own Video Academy to anyone wanting to make promotional videos." Joey Islam, programme manager

"It's been really incredible the amount of content that's been packed into this two-day course. Everything is covered – all the technical knowledge to allow a business to create videos to give themselves a professional presence." John Griffiths, web developer

"I found the course really interactive and I think the trainers are absolutely brilliant, engaging and very personable. I have got a lot from it – it was amazing to put a video together. I'm really excited to go and make my own videos and I'd actually like to come back on the advanced course as well." Nancy Lillington, fundraising manager

"Video is everywhere so I need to get some on the internet, LinkedIn, Instagram, Facebook etc. I would definitely recommend Make Your Own Video Training Academy to others. There are so many of us out there that want to share our message so we need to step up and shine and get our videos on the internet. Text is great, but video is better!" Amy Armstrong, executive coach

Make Your Own Video Training Academy Handbook

Copyright © 2017 Make Your Own Video Training Academy Ltd

www.myovdo.com
info@myovdo.com

ISBN: 978-1-9997013-0-7

First published in Great Britain by Make Your Own Video Training Academy Ltd

Set and designed by Anna Green at Siulen Design

Make Your Own Video Training Academy Ltd is a Joint Venture Company of
Gasp Creative Ltd and Shuut Ltd. The directors are Glyn Allen and Ruth Duggal,
who assert the rights to be identified as the authors of this work.

ACKNOWLEDGEMENTS

There are a number of people whose help and guidance has enabled us to write this handbook and develop Make Your Own Video Training Academy.

Firstly, thank you to the patient and eagle-eyed Peter Heath who proofread several drafts of the handbook and is now an expert in video making as well as will writing (his day job). Thank you also to Gary Smith, MD of Advance Printwear, Bonny Parkes, Director of Morgan Parkes Recruitment, Anne Finch, Community Manager of Regus Blythe Valley and Rachel Cranney, Fundraising Manager of Birmingham Rep Theatre for allowing us to take publicity photographs at their venues. Thank you to Juliet Clare Bell, Anna Swift, Michelle James, Joey Islam, John Griffiths, Amy Armstrong, Meredith Kemp-Ghani and Nancy Lillington for being our workshop guinea pigs; their honest and constructive feedback has helped us shape and develop the workshops and hopefully they gained some useful knowledge in return. Thank you to Romany Kemp-Ghani for her modeling and sketching services. Thank you to Simon Duggal for his technical and photographic support and to Dennis Davis for a killer cover shot. Thanks also to our families for their continued support.

CONTENTS

SECTION THREE – EDITING 64

SECTION FOUR – UPLOADING 88

00:00:00

INTRODUCTION

Do you want to use video to promote your organisation, products or services, but find the cost of hiring a professional video production company prohibitive?

Do you see your competitors sharing promotional videos on social media and feel like you're being left behind?

Have you tried to make a video with your smartphone and been disappointed with the results?

If your answer to any of these questions is yes, this book is for you. The Make Your Own Video Training Academy Handbook shows you how to produce your own simple, high quality promotional videos for web and social media using your mobile device*.

Most of us now carry around at least one device capable of shooting, editing and uploading High Definition (HD) video. We're going to show you how to use your device to its full potential. With just a few additional pieces of inexpensive equipment – and some video production techniques – you can make your own promotional videos simply, quickly and regularly.

*For the purposes of this Handbook 'mobile device' refers to a smartphone or tablet using an iOS or Android operating system. We are not referring to Windows devices in this version of the Handbook.

WHY MAKE YOUR OWN VIDEOS?

You might be a sole trader, run a small business, be a creative practitioner, an aspiring vlogger, work for an organisation or want to raise funds for a charity. If you have a message to share, online video is an effective way to reach your target audience and inspire them to take action.

Whilst we firmly believe there is still very much a need and a place for professional video production, learning how to make your own videos will enable you to create short, regular videos for web and social media without the expense of hiring a production company every time.

WHAT IS MAKE YOUR OWN VIDEO TRAINING ACADEMY?

Make Your Own Video Training Academy has been set up by video production experts to help you grow your organisation through the strategic use of self-made video. This book is just one aspect of the services we offer; we also hold practical workshops and offer advanced online learning modules. We can also offer full service video production to complement your own video content – for those projects that need professional expertise and specialist filming equipment. Visit our website www.myovdo.com to find out more.

HOW TO USE THIS BOOK

This book can be used by itself as a training manual. It is set out in a logical order so it's best to follow it through from start to finish rather than dip in and out. You will get more from it, however, if you couple it with one of our practical workshops. The workshops will help you to put all this information into practice under the guidance of our expert trainers. Attending one of our workshops will give you the confidence to start making your own videos – especially if you have no

prior experience of video making. Visit www.myovdo.com/workshops to book your place.

We also encourage you to sign up to our newsletter, join our Facebook community and visit the blog for useful information on video production, video trends and video marketing – www.myovdo.com. When you're ready to progress to the next level, you can purchase advanced training modules in various aspects of video production through the website – www.myovdo.com/advanced.

WHAT YOU WILL LEARN FROM MAKE YOUR OWN VIDEO TRAINING ACADEMY

This book will teach you the basics of filming and editing short promotional videos with a mobile device such as an iPad. To make it simple we have developed a unique learning path based around a set of five video **storyboards**. The storyboards have been strategically designed to help you create videos that lead your viewers on a journey from awareness to engagement. Each storyboard can be adapted to suit any type of business or organisation, and follows a simple five-step plan resulting in a suite of five one-minute videos ideal for your website and social media channels. You will find examples of these videos at www.myovdo.com/storyboards.

By following the four sections of this book – Planning, Shooting, Editing and Uploading – you will learn practical video making techniques such as choosing a location, lighting your scene, recording clear audio, framing and composing your shots, interviewing skills, presentation techniques, the principles of video editing, uploading to social media, optimising your videos and measuring their success. You will be able to apply all these techniques to the video storyboards – or any other types of videos you want to make – to create simple yet effective promotional videos to help grow your business.

Once you have mastered the structure of these videos, you'll be able to find more storyboards for different types of videos at www.myovdo.com/storyboards.

At the back of this book you'll also find a useful glossary of video making terms for your reference. There, you'll find explanations of all the words highlighted in grey throughout the book.

By the end of the book, you will have the knowledge to make simple, high quality promotional videos with your mobile device, and share them with your target audience. Then it's over to you. Only by

putting these skills into practice will you gain the true value of the information within these pages. This is where our workshops will really help you consolidate your learning.

Once you are confident making simple videos on a mobile device, you may wish to develop your video making skills by taking our online advanced modules. They cover subjects such as video structure and strategy and advanced filming, lighting and editing techniques. Visit www.myovdo.com/advanced to find out more. We will add new advanced modules over time so check the website regularly or sign up to the newsletter to receive information straight to your inbox.

Are you ready to take control of your marketing and learn how to make your own videos? Read on.

ABOUT THE AUTHORS: GLYN ALLEN & RUTH DUGGAL

We met and started working together in 1999 at a small cable TV station in Northampton. Since then we have both worked as Producers, Directors, Camera Operators and Editors in corporate video and broadcast television. Together we still run a video production company as well as train individuals and businesses to make their own videos.

During our time as video professionals, we have seen big changes to the way videos are made and used. The world is truly digital; there has never been more opportunity to reach out to people across the globe and share your message. Technology is smaller, cheaper, faster, more powerful and more user-friendly than it has ever been. It's the perfect time to learn video production techniques and take full advantage of this digital power at your fingertips.

That's why we set up Make Your Own Video Training Academy. Our mission is to make high quality video production accessible to individuals, businesses and organisations. We want to help you tell your story and grow your business; we want to teach you how to make your own videos.

PLANNING

Making successful videos requires planning; if you don't have a clear objective for each video, you won't be able to measure its success. Planning is not just about making practical preparations for the shoot – although, of course, this is a large part. It's also about understanding your audience, creating videos that interest them, and placing them on the channels they watch. We'll show you how to plan for success using our five quick and simple video Storyboards.

EQUIPMENT

To get started on your video making journey, you need a basic filming kit. In this book we teach you how to shoot and edit five types of videos using a mobile device that you may already own, or can be bought inexpensively. We'll look in more detail at the filming device in the next chapter. In this chapter we'll explain the additional pieces of equipment you need to make your device shoot-ready.

To get the most from your learning, we recommend you have all your equipment ready before you start. There are just six essential items. You can purchase all of the items (except a filming device) through our website www.myovdo.com/shop.

- A filming device – such as a tablet or smartphone*
- A tripod
- A mount to attach your filming device to the tripod (either a smartphone mount or a tablet mount, depending on which device you're using)
- A tie clip microphone**
- A microphone extension cable
- A power extension lead

HOW TO ASSEMBLE YOUR KIT

1. Let's start with your tripod. Extend the legs of the tripod by opening the clips, pulling the legs out and closing the clips again when the legs are fully extended. Open the legs to create a stable base and set the tripod on an even surface.

2. Attach the smartphone or tablet mount to the top of the tripod. On the top of your tripod you will find a removable plate. Take this out of the tripod and screw it tightly into the bottom of the mount. Fit the plate back onto the tripod, checking it's securely fixed in place.

3. Position your device in the mount. If you are using the tablet mount, loosen the screw on the back of the mount and raise the top of the clamp. Slide the device into place then lower the clamp so it grips the device securely, then tighten the screw. If you are using the smartphone mount, simply pull up the top of the clamp (which is spring loaded), position your phone and lower the clamp for a snug grip. **Position your**

device in a horizontal, not vertical, orientation. Most tablets and smartphones have a front ('selfie') and rear camera, with the rear camera shooting higher quality footage than the front. We recommend using the rear camera where possible, although there may be occasions for shooting 'selfie' video. Attach the device to the tripod with the screen facing away from the subject (the person being filmed) if you're filming someone else, or towards you if you're filming a 'selfie'.

4. Next, attach the microphone. Your device already has an internal microphone, but the sound quality is inadequate for capturing voice from a distance. For crisp, clear audio, use the recommended tie-clip external microphone. The standard length of a tie-clip microphone lead isn't long enough for filming interviews and presentations so you'll also need a microphone extension cable. To attach the mic, take the jack plug of the extension cable and insert it into the headphone socket of your tablet. Then plug the microphone into the other end of the extension cable. The mic is then attached at chest level to the clothing of the person speaking. We'll go into more detail about this in Chapter 10.

5. Before you start filming, make sure your device is fully charged. Alternatively, connect your device to mains power via the mains extension cable whilst filming***. If your device's power lead doesn't reach the floor when the device is mounted on the tripod, tape the socket of the extension cable onto a leg of the tripod with heavy duty gaffer tape, or hang it on the hook underneath the tripod.

With just these six inexpensive items, you can shoot and edit all of the storyboard videos that will be introduced in Chapter 4. To watch a video of the equipment being assembled visit www. myovdo.com/resources. Spend some time getting to know how it all fits together so you can assemble it with confidence when you come to shoot.

* For the purposes of following this book, we recommend an iPad 4th Generation or newer, an iPhone 5 or newer, or an Android device running 4.2 Jellybean or newer.

**For older devices, you may also need a microphone adaptor to ensure compatibility with the recommended microphone. See the website www.myovdo.com/shop for details.

***Some devices don't allow mains power and a microphone to be connected at the same time.

YOUR FILMING DEVICE

There are many devices on the market that will shoot, edit and upload video, but the footage quality and editing capabilities vary from model to model so it's important to understand the optimum specifications for using a mobile device as a video production tool.

Here are the main considerations when selecting a device to use for this purpose:

OPERATING SYSTEM

For iOS devices, we recommend an iPad 4th generation or newer, or an iPhone 5 or newer. For Android devices, we recommend a smartphone or tablet running Android 4.2 Jellybean or newer*. Older models will be capable of shooting video, but the editing apps may have been updated and may no longer be compatible with older versions of iOS or Android operating systems.

DEVICE SIZE

Smartphones are great for filming because they're small and portable, but the size of the screen can prevent you

from noticing details in the background of your clips. They can also be used for editing if you're happy to work on a small screen. Tablets have a bigger screen, which means you can see more detail when you're filming and editing. Additionally, tablet versions of editing apps sometimes provide more functionality than phone versions.

STORAGE CAPACITY

This refers to the amount of gigabytes (GB) your device can hold. Video is memory hungry so you'll be able to shoot more footage in one sitting with a 64GB device than you will with 16GB. We recommend checking your device's specifications online to find out how many minutes or hours of video it will store. Also, the higher the footage quality, the more storage it uses. Some devices will allow you to increase capacity by inserting an SD card or similar but others will not, so it's best to buy as much internal storage as you can afford.

CAMERA RESOLUTION

Most devices now have high definition

(HD) cameras as standard. Some will be 1080HD and some will be 720HD. The higher the number, the better quality the video. In many cases the rear camera will be higher resolution than the front camera. Watching videos online, you may not notice much difference between 720 and 1080 footage, but if you intend to show your video in different places (including large screens), always film at the highest resolution you can. Bear in mind, however, that the higher the footage resolution, the more of your device's storage capacity it will use. We recommend a device with a minimum 16GB of internal storage.

NOTE: Every device processes video differently, resulting in a discrepancy between the file size per minute of video. On average, however, 60 seconds of 1080 video requires 150 MB of storage (10 minutes requires approx 1.5 GB).

EDITOR

If you have an iOS device, you may want to use the pre-installed video editor, iMovie. If you're using a different device, you'll need to install a third party video editing application (app). There are several free or paid editing apps available, each with different levels of functionality. The very basic apps are intended for home movie editing and not suitable for our storyboard videos. The editing app you use is, of course, a personal choice but

for Android devices we recommend Kinemaster. In Chapter 17 you'll learn more about how to choose an editing app, their common features and how to use them. At this stage we recommend installing your chosen editing app to ensure it is compatible with your device. If not, you may wish to update your device's operating system or upgrade your device.

CONNECTIVITY

You will need a good quality wifi connection for uploading your footage from your device to your cloud storage, and for publishing your finished videos on social media. Video file sizes can be large (the longer the clip, the larger the file) and may take time to upload. Be aware, also, of the security of your connection, especially if you are making videos with sensitive or confidential content. A password protected connection is advisable in these cases.

Whichever device you're using, it is important to read the manufacturer's specifications in order to understand its capabilities and limitations as a video making tool. We recommend you familiarise yourself with the main functions and features of your device before you start shooting.

* We will include Windows devices in subsequent editions of the Handbook.

GETTING TO KNOW YOUR AUDIENCE

One of the purposes of this book is to teach you how to make successful videos. Success means different things to different people; for some it represents increased sales, while for others it's about raising awareness. Whatever your aim, the first step is to understand who you're making videos for and where to find them.

The single most important factor in making a successful video is to get to know your audience. If the content and style of your videos do not appeal to your audience, you're wasting your time making them. Matching your videos to your audience makes the videos easier to find, ensures the content is relevant and makes them more engaging thus increasing the chances of their success. You may have several audiences for different products or services so it's important to understand each one.

HOW TO BUILD A VIEWER PROFILE

There are two ways to do this.

1. Create an Avatar

This method will apply if you don't already have at least one customer you would class as your ideal. Take a sheet of paper and note down all the characteristics of your target viewer/customer, then display it prominently for reference. Follow the **VIEWER** method to create your avatar:

Values – their values, beliefs and their personal and professional goals

Information – personal information such as their age, gender identity, marital status, children, where they live, occupation and job title, annual income, level of education.

Enlightenment – their sources of information such as preferred news channels, magazines and newspapers, websites and blogs, social media channels and mentors or gurus.

Worries – their common worries and challenges, especially those that you can help them overcome.

Entertainment – their entertainment and leisure choices such as social activities, hobbies and interests, preferred holiday destinations, favourite films and TV shows, music tastes.

Retail habits – what they spend their money on and how much, favourite brands, online/offline shopping behaviour

When you have finished your profile, note down what style of videos you think might appeal to your target viewer. Consider aspects such as style (humorous/factual/corporate/funky etc), pace (punchy or steady), style of music and how the information is presented (as an interview, someone speaking to camera or voice-over). As a further exercise, find some online videos you think they will like and save them for reference.

2. Model An Existing Customer

If you already have at least one customer you consider your ideal, use them as your model. You will already know some of the characteristics listed above, so note them down on your profile. If there are characteristics you don't yet know – and you think learning them is important for creating relevant video content – ask your client if they would be happy to fill out a short survey to help you understand them better. It's particularly important to find out what social media channels they use, what style and type of video content they prefer, what films or TV shows they like and what brands they identify with. When you have the results of your survey you can complete your viewer profile. Again,

note down the style of videos you think your target viewer will enjoy.

Repeat this process for different audiences. For further guidance on building a viewer profile, book a one-to-one consultation with us by visiting www.myovdo.com/shop or come along to one of our workshops, which can be booked at www.myovdo.com/workshop.

BUILD A VIEWER PROFILE

PERSONAL INFORMATION

- Age
- Gender identity
- Marital status
- Children?
- Location
- Occupation/ title
- Annual income
- Education
- Religion

40 years old
Male
Married
2 children
50 miles of Birmingham – village in countryside
Marketing Director.

GOALS, VALUES & CHALLENGES

- Personal/ professional goals

- Values

- Challenges

SOURCES OF INFO

nels

nels

4

VIDEO STORYBOARDS

In this chapter we're helping you to plan a video strategy. What does this mean? It means we're giving you suggestions about what types of videos to use at the different stages of your customers'* journey.

We have created five simple and adaptable video storyboards that you can easily follow to make five different types of videos – videos that are commonly used by businesses and organisations to promote their services and raise awareness. They can be used on different pages of your website and on your social media channels. The beauty of these storyboards is that they can be adapted to suit the nature of your business, organisation or offering.

Each storyboard follows a simple five-step plan. They provide a quick and easy way to get you started on your video making journey, and you will learn all the skills to make them through this Handbook. You can also purchase more storyboards for other types of videos from www.myovdo. com/storyboards.

The storyboards are divided into two columns: the 'script' is the information you want to share and the 'footage' is what the viewer will see. Don't worry if you're unclear at this stage how to present the information and what to film; we will work through various filming techniques and terminologies in the following chapters and you can refer back to the storyboards when you're ready to start shooting. We have also included approximate timings for each step, which are to be used as a guide only.

* By 'customer' we refer to your target viewer; you might call them something different depending on the nature of your business or organisation.

Visit www.myovdo.com/resources to download a blank PDF storyboard you can fill in yourself and to see examples of all of these videos, filmed and edited on mobile devices. You will also find more storyboards for many other types of videos, which can be purchased individually.

STORYBOARD #1 **The Overview**

The Overview provides a flavour of what you do or offer. Its function is to attract the attention of passing viewers, whetting their appetite for more information. It shows the benefits, rather than the features of the service you offer, answering the inevitable question, "Why should I care about you?" Use this video on the homepage of your website, and on social media channels where viewers are searching for a solution to their problems.

STEP 1 (10 seconds)	SCRIPT	FOOTAGE
	In one sentence, describe what it means to you to see customers gaining benefit from your services.	Supplementary footage of customers OR Person talking AND Name caption
STEP 2 (10 seconds)	**SCRIPT**	**FOOTAGE**
	Briefly describe what motivates you or your organisation to do what you do.	Person talking AND Name caption (if not already shown)
STEP 3 (10 seconds)	**SCRIPT**	**FOOTAGE**
	In one sentence, describe what services you offer.	Person talking OR Supplementary footage of products/ services
STEP 4 (20 seconds)	**SCRIPT**	**FOOTAGE**
	Describe what benefits your customers receive from using your services.	Person talking OR Supplementary footage of your customers using products/services
STEP 5 (10 seconds)	**SCRIPT**	**FOOTAGE**
	State your call to action (e.g. watch another video, contact us, visit us, like, share etc)	Person talking OR Supplementary footage of more products/services/premises AND Information on screen

STORYBOARD #2 **The Explainer**

The Explainer is for viewers who are interested in your offering and want to know more. It provides more details about a specific product or service – make separate videos for each one. It describes the features and benefits of the service, and answers the question, "How does this product/service solve my problem?" Use these videos on separate pages of your website, and on your social media channels with relevant titles and descriptions.

STEP 1 (10 seconds)	SCRIPT	FOOTAGE
	State the product/service you're going to explain, e.g. "In this video I'm going to talk about…"	Person talking AND Name caption
STEP 2 (10 seconds)	SCRIPT	FOOTAGE
	State briefly why you think an explanation is important/necessary and what the viewer will gain from watching it.	Person talking OR Supplementary footage of the product/service
STEP 3 (10 seconds)	SCRIPT	FOOTAGE
	Explain the product/service step-by-step	Person talking OR Supplementary footage of product/ service being used
STEP 4 (20 seconds)	SCRIPT	FOOTAGE
	What benefits do your customers receive from using this product/ service?	Person talking OR Supplementary footage of you or a customer using the service
STEP 5 (10 seconds)	SCRIPT	FOOTAGE
	State your call to action (e.g. watch another video, contact us, buy the product/service etc)	Person talking AND Information on screen

STORYBOARD #3 **The Personal Introduction**

The Personal Introduction is an opportunity for your customers to get to know the people behind the brand. It isn't about selling a product or service; it's about showing your customers you're authentic and have a genuine passion for what you do. People buy from people, so have fun and show them your human side. Make one video for each person in your organisation. Put them on the Team page of your website and use it on your LinkedIn and AboutMe profile. You can also use them in your email signature – visit www. myovdo.com for the advanced module in using videos in emails.

STEP 1 (10 seconds)	SCRIPT	FOOTAGE
	Tell viewers who you are and what your role is	Person talking AND Name caption
STEP 2 (10 seconds)	**SCRIPT**	**FOOTAGE**
	Describe what you love about your job	Person talking OR Supplementary footage of the person at work
STEP 3 (10 seconds)	**SCRIPT**	**FOOTAGE**
	Share an interesting fact or anecdote about yourself that people will remember	Person talking OR Supplementary footage or images related to the anecdote, if available OR Supplementary footage of the person in relaxed mode
STEP 4 (20 seconds)	**SCRIPT**	**FOOTAGE**
	Your personal motto or mission statement	Person talking OR Supplementary footage of the person writing their motto and holding it up to camera
STEP 5 (10 seconds)	**SCRIPT**	**FOOTAGE**
	State your call to action such as: • Contact me directly • Watch videos of other team members • Watch another video about our company • Email us • Arrange a meeting	Person talking AND Information on screen

STORYBOARD #4 **The How-to**

"How to..." is the most commonly used search term on the internet. If there's something useful you can show viewers how to do, you will not only capitalise on this search trend, but also show your viewers your expertise in a particular area... thus increasing your credibility. Also, the perception that you're giving away 'free' information increases your likeability. How-to videos are common on social media channels. You can also use them on your blog, in your newsletters and on relevant pages of your website.

STEP 1 (10 seconds)	SCRIPT	FOOTAGE
	Describe in one sentence what this video is about	Person talking AND Name caption

STEP 2 (10 seconds)	SCRIPT	FOOTAGE
	Describe why you're making this video and what qualifies you to do so.	Person talking OR Relevant supplementary footage

STEP 3 (10 seconds)	SCRIPT	FOOTAGE
	Talk through the instructions in bullet points, as briefly as possible	Person talking OR Supplementary footage of you demonstrating how to... (close-up shots)

STEP 4 (20 seconds)	SCRIPT	FOOTAGE
	Invite your audience to try it for themselves	Person talking OR Supplementary footage of someone trying it

STEP 5 (10 seconds)	SCRIPT	FOOTAGE
	Call to action: tell your audience where they can find more hints and tips/information/contact you	Person talking AND Information on screen

STORYBOARD #5 **The Testimonial**

Testimonial videos are widely used by businesses and organisations to influence the behaviour of viewers. They are videos of your happy customers endorsing your products or services and sharing their positive customer experience. If your prospective customers have made it this far along the buyer's journey, a testimonial video can be the factor that persuades them to make a commitment. It is usually easy to find customers who are willing to appear on camera in this capacity, especially if you have made a positive impact on their lives. Testimonial videos work particularly well on websites as well as selected social media channels.

STEP 1 (10 seconds)	SCRIPT	FOOTAGE
	Introduce yourself. How has this product/service/ organisation impacted on or changed your life?	Person talking AND Name caption
STEP 2 (10 seconds)	**SCRIPT**	**FOOTAGE**
	What problem did you have, and why was it important to find a solution?	Person talking OR Supplementary footage
STEP 3 (10 seconds)	**SCRIPT**	**FOOTAGE**
	How has the company/product/ service solved your problem?	Person talking OR Supplementary footage of company/ products/services
STEP 4 (20 seconds)	**SCRIPT**	**FOOTAGE**
	Are there any aspects of the customer service you received that deserve a special mention and why?	Person talking OR Supplementary footage of person mentioned
STEP 5 (10 seconds)	**SCRIPT**	**FOOTAGE**
	How likely are you to recommend the company/product/service to others?	Person talking AND Information on screen

5

HOW TO DELIVER YOUR MESSAGE

There are several ways to deliver information through video, and it's advisable to start thinking about this during the planning stage. In this chapter we're looking at three common methods: interview, presentation **and** voice-over. **The method you choose will depend on the type of information you're delivering, and what you think your audience would prefer. All of these methods can be used in conjunction with the video storyboards.**

INTERVIEWS

An interview is where the person in front of the camera (also called the 'subject') responds to questions asked by an interviewer positioned off-camera. The subject is usually positioned to either the left or right of the video frame speaking to an interviewer on the opposite side of the camera. You'll find information on how to set up for an interview in the Resources section of our website. Here are some pros and cons of the interview method:

PROS

- Interviews are ideal for testimonials and overviews
- They encourage a natural and authentic form of delivery – a conversation rather than a presentation
- They are better suited to people who lack confidence in front of a camera
- They can seem more sincere than a presentation
- There's no need to memorise a script beforehand

CONS

- Interviews are not suitable for all types of videos – especially instructional videos
- The subject might be uncomfortable in front of the camera
- The subject might ramble, or give one-word answers
- The interviewer needs to learn interview techniques beforehand
- If you are the person being interviewed, you'll need to find someone else to ask the questions

In Chapter 13 we will give you techniques for conducting effective interviews.

PRESENTATIONS

A presentation is where the subject talks directly to the viewer through the camera lens. If you've never done this before it can take a bit of confidence and practice. Here are some pros and cons to consider:

PROS

- Presentations are great for giving advice, instructions, information and tips
- They can feel intimate and authoritative
- You are connecting directly with your viewer
- They can portray you as a trusted authority

CONS

- Presentations are not suited to all types of videos – such as testimonials or some videos of an emotional nature
- They can come across as 'preachy' or patronising if you don't get the delivery right
- They're not ideal for people who lack confidence in front of a camera
- You have to know exactly what you want to say beforehand, or memorise a script
- It can be tricky to keep your eyes on the camera lens through the whole video, especially if you're using the 'selfie' camera
- If you've never done it before, you'll need to practise presentation skills

In Chapter 14 we share some useful tips and techniques for presenting to camera.

VOICE-OVER

A voice-over is where you hear a voice but don't see the person speaking. Instead, you see footage relevant to the words you're hearing. Voice-over videos are ideal if your subject matter is particularly visual. Here are some pros and cons to consider:

PROS

- Voice-over videos are great if you are able to shoot plenty of visual content such as products, a shop, a salon, or a property
- They're great for explaining a technical process, or step by step instructions
- You don't have to memorise a script – you can simply read it
- It's much quicker to record a voice-over than film an interview or presentation
- Voice-over is perfect if you're camera-shy

CONS

- You have to be certain you can film enough relevant footage to fill the video, otherwise there will be blank spaces in your video
- Voice-over isn't suitable for explaining a service or recounting an event that has already happened (because you may not be able to shoot enough footage)

- Your voice may not be suitable for voice-over (but you can improve with practice)
- Voice-overs are not suitable for very long videos – unless you have enough footage
- It might feel too impersonal for certain types of videos

If you've never recorded a voice-over before, it can take practice to make it sound natural, confident and un-read. In Chapter 21 we'll explain how to record a voice-over and edit it into a video.

There are other ways to present the information in your videos. You may wish to explore these methods in our advanced training modules. Visit www.myovdo.com/advanced to find out more.

6

HOW TO CHOOSE A FILMING LOCATION

A big part of planning for your video is finding a suitable place to shoot. You may already have a location in mind – it could be a corner of your office or a room at home. You'll probably want to select a location based on its relevance to the subject matter of the video you're shooting, but if your location doesn't meet certain practical criteria, it might be difficult to film there. Follow our SPACES guide to assess the suitability of a filming location:

SPACE

You need enough space for your filming equipment and your subject. If you want to film just their head and shoulders you'll need less space than if you want to film them full length because the camera will need to be further away. We recommend a minimum distance between the camera and the subject of 1.3 metres. You'll also need space between your subject and the background, taking into account any elements you want visible in your video frame. If you're planning

to make regular videos, you might want to create your own permanent backdrop and we have created an advanced module to help you do this. Visit www. myovdo.com/advanced.

PERMISSION

If you intend to shoot anywhere that you don't own – whether that's on a public street, or in a privately owned building – it's always best to seek permission from the owner before you film.

ACCESS

Consider how easy it will be to reach the location; if you're driving, you'll need to park nearby and if you're using public transport it'll need to be close to a train station or bus stop. If you're filming someone who will struggle with the stairs, use a ground floor area or ensure the location has an elevator. Also check whether there are any scheduled events or roadworks around the location that could prevent you reaching it or causing noise disruption.

CLEAR LIGHTING

In this book we're showing you how to make best use of available light sources, rather than using a video lighting kit. 'Available light' means natural light from windows, and artificial lighting such as angled lamps. Find a location that has a decent source of natural light from a window and use this to light your subject (not as a background for the reason mentioned below). We will go into more detail about how to use natural light and top up with artificial lighting in Chapter 9.

ENVIRONMENT

The environment, or background should be relevant to the subject matter of your video. There are, however, certain things it's best to avoid filming in front of. Never position your subject in front of a window because they'll become a silhouette. Reflective surfaces should also be avoided, unless you want the camera operator to make a cameo appearance. Remove any rubbish or clutter that will give the viewer a negative impression. Avoid plants or tall objects that appear to be 'growing' out of your subject's head. Narrow pull-up banners are also unsuitable because they don't fit the horizontal dimensions of a video frame. Avoid any unsuitable or wordy signage and remove anything of a confidential or copyright protected nature.

SOUND

The quieter your location to start with, the better. Go into the space you're planning to use and listen. You may hear **continuous** sounds such as electrical hums and whirrs, ticking clocks, general traffic noises, heating systems and air conditioning units. There may also be **intermittent** sounds like bleepers or alarms, people talking, walking, banging doors, phones or bells, tannoy announcements, roadworks, horns, sirens or dogs barking.

Try to eliminate as many of these sounds as possible, especially if they're particularly loud and distracting. Close doors and windows, film at quieter times of day, put up 'Filming in Progress' signs and ask people to move around quietly, turn off electrical equipment, switch mobiles to silent and unplug landlines. If you think the noise level will be too difficult to control and will spoil your video, look for a different location.

Check also for echo, as too much can make your audio impossible to hear. A space with soft furnishings will be better than an empty room with hard floors.

7

FINAL PREPARATIONS FOR THE SHOOT

We've almost reached the end of the Planning section. Before we move on, follow the VIDEOS check-list to help make sure you have everything ready for the shoot.

VIDEO CONTENT

Check the storyboard and script to ensure you are happy with the content and how you are going to deliver it (interview, presentation or voice-over). Make sure your contributors or subjects are comfortable with what you'd like them to say.

INSTRUCTIONS

If there are more people involved than just you, provide instructions such as location, start time, and any transport, parking or access information.

DRESS CODE

At the same time, let your subjects know what they should and shouldn't wear. The general rule for filming is no fine stripes or checks (they may cause glare) avoid very bright or very dark colours, no jingly jewellery that could make a distracting noise and wear separates or a jacket for ease of attaching the microphone.

EQUIPMENT

Check you have all the right pieces of equipment (see Chapter 1), that you have enough storage space on your device for new footage and that the battery is fully charged.

OBTAIN PERMISSIONS

Remember, if you want to film on public or privately owned land or property, seek the owner's permission first.

SIGNATURE

If someone other than you is appearing in your video, it's advisable to get their signed consent that they're happy to take part. Do this during the shoot, but prepare your consent form in advance. Download an example of a consent form from **www.myovdo.com/resources**.

And that's it, you're ready to roll. In the next section we'll show you step by step how to film your videos.

SHOOTING

"Action!" This is the fun part where you put your preparations into practice. As you will discover, there are several aspects to consider when shooting a video: background, framing, lighting, sound, interviewing and presenting. If you're filming as well as starring in your own videos, you'll be the director, producer, set designer *and* presenter. Once you're confident with each aspect, start to use your creativity and have some fun. Follow the Storyboards to guide you through the shooting process.

8

SETTING UP FOR THE SHOOT

In section one, you prepared your filming equipment, got to know your audience, planned your video strategy using the storyboards, learnt about the different ways to deliver your information and found a suitable filming location. In this section we're ready to start shooting.

For the purposes of putting your learning into practice as you go, select a storyboard you'd like to work on and decide on your method of delivery. If you're using the presentation or voice-over methods, write your script following the five steps. If you've decided to interview someone, we'll give you some tips for conducting interviews in Chapter 13.

Now you're ready to set up your equipment for the shoot. Here's a handy reference guide for you to follow:

1. Set up your filming kit as described in Chapter 1. To recap, your kit consists of a filming device such as an iPad, a tripod, a mount to attach your device to the tripod, a tie clip microphone, a microphone extension cable and a mains extension lead.

TIP: set the filming device in a horizontal, not vertical orientation. Switch it to aeroplane mode so you don't receive distracting alerts whilst shooting.

2. Once your kit is set, take a look around your space and decide which way you want to shoot. Remember, use the window as a light source not as a background. Leave space between the subject and the background, and the camera and the subject. If you want to film your subject full length, you'll need more space than if you only want to film their head and shoulders. We'll look at how to frame your subject in more detail in Chapter 11.

TIP: if you want your subject closer to the camera, physically move the camera closer to your subject rather than using the in-camera zoom tool. Digital zoom on mobile devices reduces the picture quality the more you zoom, so move the camera, not the zoom.

3. Set the height of your camera for the height of your subject by raising or lowering the tripod. Your device should be positioned at the same level as your subject's eyes so they are looking straight on rather than

up or down. If you are interviewing your subject, the interviewer's eyes will also need to be at the same level as the camera so that your subject's eyeline is level with theirs as well as with the camera.

4. If you'd prefer your subject to sit rather than stand, it's important to choose the right chair. The type of seat can make a big difference to how your subject looks and performs. The best type of seat is a stool or high-backed chair, which will encourage the subject to sit upright or lean slightly towards the camera. If they're on a low, comfortable sofa, they will automatically lean backwards and bring their knees up, placing their lower body at the forefront of the frame – not their most flattering angle!

Now you're ready to set your lighting. We'll show you how to do this in the next chapter.

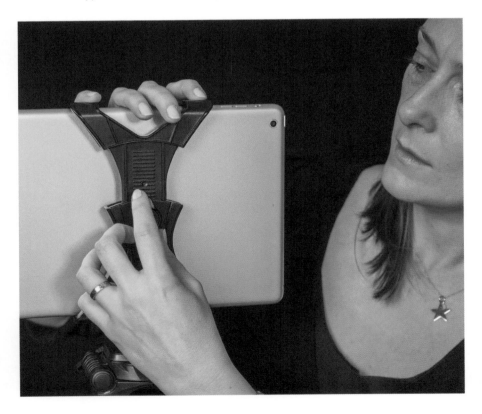

9

HOW TO LIGHT YOUR SCENE

For simple videos, you don't need an expensive video lighting kit to illuminate your scene. In this chapter we're going to show you how to make the best use of light sources already available. There are two types of available light: natural light from a window and artificial light from lamps and ceiling lights. Start with natural light if it's available, then top up with artificial light if necessary. Your aim is to achieve evenly balanced lighting conditions.

Follow these steps to achieve a pleasant lighting effect:

1. It helps if your location has a good source of natural light. Set your filming kit so the light source comes from behind or slightly to the side of the camera, illuminating your subject's face.
2. Different weather conditions will result in different intensities of light. If it's a bright day, try moving your subject further away from the window to spread out, or diffuse, the light. If it's still too bright, try closing blinds or curtains a little. You might find it useful to get a piece of sheer fabric such as a voile curtain to tape to the window frame, which will help to diffuse the light.
3. You might be happy with the natural lighting alone. If not, top up with artificial light. Ceiling lights provide an overall brightness, and the higher the ceiling the more evenly the light will spread. Avoid fluorescent striplights, which buzz and flicker, and low halogen spots as they can create a sinister effect!
4. The best type of artificial light is an anglepoise lamp because you can move it around and direct the light where you want it. Experiment with distance – move it closer to your subject for intense lighting or further away for a softer look. Move it to the opposite side from the natural light source to even out the overall light, or angle it upwards to bounce the light off the ceiling for a more diffused look.
5. Experiment with different lighting conditions to achieve the desired effect. If you plan to shoot many videos in the same space, make a note of the light setup once you're happy with it, so you can recreate it on a different day.

TIP: Take a photo of your lighting setup for future reference.

10

RECORDING CLEAR AUDIO

In this chapter we're looking at how to capture clear audio during the shoot. Achieving good, clear sound is important because it's one of the key differentiators between amateur and high quality video. Remember, audio is fifty percent of your video. If someone is talking, you want to be able to hear them clearly with minimal background interference. This is why we recommend using an external microphone that plugs into your filming device.

1. Take steps to minimise any continuous or intermittent noises, as described in Chapter 6.
2. Use the recommended external mic, not the device's internal microphone, when filming interviews, presentations and voice-overs. The sound quality will be far superior.
3. Attach the microphone to your subject. To keep your shot tidy, hide the cable under your subject's clothing. Separates are easier than one-piece dresses for this. Ask your subject to feed the mic under their top and bring it out of the neck hole, or hide the cable inside a jacket. If they're wearing a button-through shirt, bring the mic out between the buttons about two or three down. Use the clip that comes with the mic to clip it on to the neckline, lapel, button strip or tie. Then pull any excess cable down at the bottom so the mic is sitting neatly against the clothing without pulling the garment out of shape.
4. Remove any jewellery such as necklaces, brooches, dangly earrings, or lanyards that could tap against the microphone. Additionally, remove bangles or bracelets that could jingle as your subject gesticulates.
5. Before you start filming, check the sound level by recording a short clip of your subject counting from one to ten at their normal volume. Unplug the mic then play back the clip with the volume up to max. If it's too quiet, move the mic closer to the subject's mouth and ask them to speak a little louder. If it's too loud it will sound distorted or 'fuzzy'. Move the mic further away from the subject's mouth and ask them to speak a little quieter.
6. Finally, avoid any unwanted interruptions by asking everyone present to turn their phones to silent. If you're using yours for filming, turn it to aeroplane mode.

11

FRAMING AND COMPOSING YOUR SHOTS

Good composition is about the balance of elements within the video frame, with the main subject taking precedence. Traditionally video has been shot and viewed in a horizontal orientation (also described as 16:9), but there's a growing trend towards square (1:1) and vertical (9:16) video formats on social media channels. In this chapter we're focussing on framing and composing for horizontal and square videos; we'll keep you updated on developments in vertical video through our newsletter, blog and social media channels.

THE RULE OF FRAMING

This is about how much of your subject is visible in the frame. There are several types of shots within this rule, and we've provided suggestions on how and when to use them.

1. **Long Shot** – this is where the entire subject is visible from head to feet. This type of shot is usually used to establish where the video is set, if it's important to do so.

2. **Medium Shot** – in this shot the subject is visible from the waist up, with comfortable space around the top of the head. This is a good type of shot for a presentation or instructional video.

3. **Medium Close Up** – in this type of shot the subject is visible from about the chest upwards, again with comfortable space around the head. This is the most common type of shot for interviews.

4. **Close Up** – in this shot only the subject's head and shoulders are visible. This is an intimate shot, usually used to emphasise a point or an emotion. You can also couple it with the Medium close-up to add variety and interest to an interview.

5. **Extreme Close Up** – in this type of shot only one part of the subject fills the frame – for example the eyes or hands. This shot can be used if you need additional footage to cover a join in your edit, or to show something in more detail.

Alternating the framing throughout your video can make it more interesting for the viewer, especially if your video contains just one person talking. For example, when you're following one of the storyboards and two consecutive steps feature the same person talking, shoot step one medium close-up and step two close-up. When you edit the sections together, the video will cut smoothly between the two framings without a 'jump' effect.

THE RULE OF THIRDS

Use this in conjunction with the Rule of Framing to achieve well composed shots. This rule traditionally applies to horizontal video, but it can be applied to square video as well. Imagine splitting your video frame into equal thirds horizontally, then equal thirds vertically. Studies have shown that the viewer's eyes are drawn naturally to one of the intersecting points or along the lines – rather than to the centre.

So, when filming a person, frame them so their eyes are positioned along the upper line or at one of the upper intersection points. When filming buildings, position them along either of the two vertical lines instead of in the centre. Any other elements in the background can be arranged to balance with the subject. Position them along the opposite lines or intersection points for an evenly balanced shot.

SHOOTING FOR SQUARE VIDEO

If you look at channels such as Facebook and Instagram, you'll notice the area in which images and videos can be displayed is square, not rectangular. Whilst it is possible to place horizontal video in a square window, valuable space is lost at the top and bottom of the frame. If you know your target audience is using channels with square viewing windows, you may wish to consider filling all of the available space with valuable video content.

When shooting for square video, you'll be setting up your device in the same way you would to shoot horizontal video, but your subject and any important action must be positioned in one area of the frame, such as the centre, left or right. You may find it useful to create a square aperture out of paper that you can position over your screen, to ensure any important action is taking place within the square frame and will not be lost during the cropping process.

We'll look at how to edit and crop square videos in the editing section. Follow our blog and subscribe to our newsletter to receive information on the latest trends in online video www.myovdo.com.

12

FOCUS AND APERTURE

It's worth spending a bit of time at this stage understanding focus and aperture. Focus is about being able to see your image clearly without it being fuzzy or blurry. The aperture is the hole through which light passes into the camera. The hole can be opened or closed to make your image brighter or darker.

be the most important part of the frame.

In situations like this, it's easy to override the autofocus to ensure your subject is crystal clear. All you need to do is tap and hold the screen on your subject, and the camera will lock focus on that point. Regardless of what's going on behind, your subject will remain in focus until you stop recording.

FOCUS

If you're using your device's standard camera app, the focus is set to automatic. This means the camera will automatically focus on what it perceives to be the main subject of the frame. However, there may be occasions when the autofocus will let you down and you'll end up with a blurry image, so it's useful to know how to focus your camera manually.

The most likely situations where defocusing will occur is if you have a deep background, if there's a lot of background activity, or if the background is brighter than the foreground. This will be compounded if your subject remains relatively still, even though they're at the front of the frame. The camera will automatically focus on what it deems to

APERTURE

Again, if you're using your device's standard camera app, the aperture is also set to automatic. You may find in certain situations, however, that even though you can clearly see the scene with your naked eye, the view through your camera is too dark or too bright. If your scene is not evenly lit – for example if there is more light on one side of the screen than the other – the camera will automatically set the aperture to the brightest part of the scene, making the rest of it dark.

There are two ways to remedy this. Firstly, try introducing another lamp to brighten the darker area of the scene. Secondly, open the aperture on your camera by tapping on the screen at the darkest point until you see a small box with a lightbulb or sun symbol next to it. Slide the symbol up or down to lighten or darken the image as desired.

There are third party camera apps available from your app store (iOS and Android) that provide more control over focus and aperture. For an advanced module in how to use these, visit the website www.myovdo.com/advanced.

13

HOW TO CONDUCT EFFECTIVE INTERVIEWS

In this chapter we're looking at how to set your subject at ease and achieve good quality responses that serve the purpose of your video. If you're using the video storyboards from Chapter 4, you'll find they already include suggested interview questions to guide you through the process.

Here are the 10 Is of getting the best from your interviewee:

Interviewee – speak to your interviewee in advance of filming, especially if you don't already know them, to find out how they feel about being interviewed. Set them at ease by explaining what will happen and approximately how long it will take.

Inform – on the day of the interview, make your subject feel comfortable by informing them what will happen, offering them a glass of water and explaining that they can repeat a response if they're not happy with the first take.

Introduce – at the start of the interview, ask your subject to introduce him or herself by stating their full name and title, including the spelling; you'll need this when you create a name caption during the editing process.

Incorporate – ask your subject to incorporate your question in their answer so that you can edit out the interviewer's question and the response will still make sense. For example, when you ask, "How likely are you to recommend this product to others?" you want them to say, "I am very likely to recommend this product", rather than just, "Very", otherwise the audience won't know what they mean. They may forget to do this as the interview progresses, so it's okay to keep reminding them.

Don't **interrupt** – don't talk over your subject or interrupt them. Wait until they have completely finished speaking before you ask the next question.

Influence their delivery – if your interviewee isn't responding in a way that fits the style of your video – for example they sound flat or way too happy – alter the way you communicate with them to encourage them to mirror your behaviour.

Intention – listen carefully to their response to ensure that what they have said serves the purpose or intention of your video.

In a nutshell – try to get shorter versions if their first response is too long. Do this by asking the following: "If you were to sum up that last response in one sentence, how would you do it?"

Impact – if your subject's responses sound scripted, they'll have less impact than if they're natural. Be wary of giving your subject the interview questions in advance of filming. If you do, ask them to prepare bullet points rather than a script.

Improve – if it has taken several questions for your subject to relax and provide useful responses, round off the interview by asking the first few questions again – you'll probably notice an improvement in their answers.

In the Resources area of our website you'll find an illustration of how to position your equipment for shooting an interview.

14

HOW TO PRESENT TO CAMERA

Presenting to a camera doesn't come naturally to everyone, so if you'd like to present your own videos but aren't sure where to start, this chapter provides techniques used by professionals to deliver a confident, authentic and engaging presentation.

Follow the 10 Ps of presenting to achieve an accomplished delivery:

Perception – the most important tip is to be yourself. If your viewers' perception of you is false they will struggle to find you authentic.

Prepare – learn your script. It doesn't look good if you have to keep glancing away from the camera lens to read a sheet of paper. Knowing your script will help you deliver it with confidence.

Progression – if you're using the storyboards, they are divided into five steps so it's easy to film them one by one, repeating each one as many times as it takes to achieve a delivery you're happy with.

Point of view – get used to looking and talking into the camera lens. On a mobile device the lens is a very small circle, so make sure you know your point of view before you start shooting.

Position – anchor yourself in one position. If you're standing, place your feet a comfortable distance apart and keep them there. Put a marker on the floor and stay on that spot. This will prevent you from shuffling around and appearing nervous. If you are sitting, use an upright chair with your feet touching the floor.

Pace – speak at a steady pace. Before you start, take some deep breaths, then make sure you keep breathing throughout your presentation. Don't race through your script because your audience will find it difficult to keep up.

Pause – once you've hit record, position yourself as though you're ready to start speaking, but pause for a few seconds before you do. Similarly when you've finished speaking, continue looking into the camera for a few seconds before you hit stop. This will give you space – or 'handles' – at either end of your clip to make it easier for editing.

Presence – Think about your body language – stand confidently with your shoulders back and your arms relaxed. Use your hands to gesticulate if it feels natural to do so. If not, either keep your arms by your sides, or on your lap if you're sitting.

Be **positive** – smile before you speak. It will help you to deliver a positive and sincere presentation.

Practise – finally, practise each script before you start shooting, and practise all of these techniques so you become confident and comfortable presenting to camera.

TIP: when you shoot your clips, mark each scene with a visual reference such as a sheet of paper stating the section/scene number. This will make it easier for you to find individual clips when you edit your footage. To mark a clip, press record then hold the sheet up to the camera for a few seconds before you deliver your script.

15

SHOOTING SUPPLEMENTARY FOOTAGE

Supplementary footage is additional content that enhances your interview or presentation to help tell the story in a visual way. It is filmed after your interview or presentation and added to your video during the editing process. It should be absolutely relevant to the subject matter so it does not confuse or mislead the viewer.

Always shoot your interview or presentation first, so you know exactly what has been said, and therefore what supplementary footage you will need. If you're making a voice-over video, it will consist entirely of supplementary footage; write your script first, shoot your supplementary footage and then record the voice-over during the editing process – we'll show you how in Chapter 21.

Here's how to shoot supplementary footage:

1. Create a shot list
A shot list is a written list of the different shots (or clips) you need to supplement your interview, presentation or voice-over. If you have filmed using a storyboard, you may have already noted down what supplementary footage you need in the 'Footage' column. If you have filmed an interview, your subject may have said some things you didn't expect, so play back the interview and note down what additional footage you need.

2. Framing
On your shot list also note down your desired framing of each supplementary shot. Refer back to the Rule Of Framing in Chapter 11 to help you. For example, if you have filmed a 'How To' video you may want to capture extreme close up shots of an object; for an 'Overview' video you might film a long shot of an office, followed by medium or close up shots of individuals at work. If you are shooting for square video, remember to position all the important action in one area of the frame, such as the centre, left or right. This must be the same area in which you positioned your presenter or interviewee, as you will be cropping the entire video during the editing process.

3. Movement
Adding movement to your supplementary footage can help your video to flow

nicely. It's best to use a tripod so the moves are steady, not shaky. A **pan** is a movement of the camera from left to right (or vice versa) from a fixed position – like standing on one spot and turning your head one way or the other. Pan shots are useful if you want to show a wide area that doesn't fit into the frame. A **tilt** is a movement of the camera up or down from a fixed position – like standing on one spot and nodding your head. Tilt shots are good for showing things that are taller than your frame such as buildings. Moves should be kept to a steady speed – you don't want to give your viewers motion sickness!

4. Length

The length of your supplementary shots will depend on the length of dialogue with which you plan to use them. Always make your supplementary shots slightly longer than the passage of dialogue, to give you space for precision editing. You'll see why this is important when you reach the editing section of the book.

5. Lighting

Your supplementary footage should be as well-lit as your interviews or presentations, so it's worth going back over the lighting chapter (Chapter 9) and applying the same methods to this footage.

6. Audio

Supplementary footage doesn't usually require sound because you'll probably be using the audio from your interview, presentation or voice-over. Therefore, there's no need to connect your external microphone for these shots. Your device will capture background audio with its internal mic, and you can use this sound quietly in the background of your video to add atmosphere, if required.

16

BACKING UP YOUR FOOTAGE

Once you have shot your footage the next step is to store it safely, regardless of whether or not you intend to edit and upload it straight away. It's good practice to establish a storage and back-up system for all your source **footage and edited videos.**

When using a single device for filming and editing, you'll need a backup system separate from the device otherwise you'll quickly run out of space for new footage. The simplest solution, regardless of what device or operating system you're using, is cloud storage. Cloud storage is space reserved for data on remote servers, accessed through the internet.

Popular cloud storage solutions include Google Photos and Dropbox, all of which are compatible with iOS and Android devices. Such solutions usually offer free accounts with limited amounts of storage (some more than others). Due to the size of video files, however, you may find it necessary to upgrade to a paid plan. Check with the individual providers for storage capacity, plans and pricing.

There are two ways to backup your footage to the cloud. Before you do,

you'll first need to create a cloud storage account following the instructions of your chosen provider. Once set up, you can use one of the following methods:

1. Set your device to automatically back-up your photos and videos to your preferred cloud storage provider (consult your device's instructions). Set it to upload in full (or original) resolution. Once set, any photos or videos you take on your device will automatically back up to the cloud whenever your device is connected to wifi.

OR

2. Manually upload your footage from within the cloud storage app. Your device must be connected to wifi in order to do this. Load the app, create a new folder or album for your footage then tap 'Upload' or the plus icon. Select all the clips you'd like to backup then tap 'Upload'. Wait for the clips to upload.

Do not delete any footage from your device until you are certain it has completely backed up to the cloud. To check the progress of the backup, open your cloud storage app. If you can't see the individual clips in the cloud folder, they haven't uploaded yet. Of course, you won't want to delete the footage until after you have edited it anyway. In Chapter 23 we will show you how to backup your edited videos to cloud storage as well.

Once you've backed up your footage, you're ready to start editing. In the next section of the book we'll show you how.

EDITING

Editing is where the magic happens; it's the process of turning your raw footage into a polished video. Don't be concerned if you have never edited before; most video editing applications work in similar ways, and once you understand the basic principles you'll be able to create good quality videos with very little need for technical know how. The best way to learn is to get hands-on. In this section you'll learn how to assemble clips into a sequence and how to embellish with effects, text and music.

UNDERSTANDING VIDEO EDITING PROGRAMMES

In this chapter we're looking at the common features of video editing programmes. There are plenty of video editing applications available to download from your app store, with differing costs and levels of functionality. For the purposes of editing your storyboard videos, however, we recommend iMovie for iOS devices (free) and Kinemaster for Android devices (free, but upgrade is recommended).

Whilst we're not providing a step-by-step guide to how these individual editing apps work, there are similarities between their interfaces. This guide will help you to recognise them and understand what each function does. The best way to learn is to jump in with some test footage and follow the app's own tutorials.

Most editing apps will have the following features:

NEW PROJECT

To edit a new video from scratch you first need to launch the editing app and create a new project. Do this by tapping the plus symbol or selecting 'New Project'. Additionally, you may need to select 'Create Movie' to access the editing interface. Your new project will automatically be given a title such as 'My Movie' or 'Untitled 1'. Rename the video by selecting the project and tapping on the existing title; delete this and type a new one.

THE EDITING INTERFACE

Once you've created a new project and opened it, you're likely to see the following features:

MEDIA BROWSER

This is the area at the top right or left of the screen from where your source footage is accessed. Tap on 'Media Browser' or 'Videos' and select the folder in which the footage from your camera is stored. You will then see still images of the clips you have filmed, arranged from latest to oldest.

VIEWER

This is located next to the media browser. It is the screen on which you can view your clips. To play a clip, tap it to highlight it then tap the play button (the triangle). In some apps you may need to tap and hold a clip in order to view it.

TIMELINE

This is the horizontal area at the bottom of the screen where you assemble your clips into a video. Select clips from the media browser and move them onto the timeline to start editing. This is done either by double tapping a clip or by highlighting it and tapping the plus symbol.

When a clip has moved to the timeline, it sits on what's called a **layer**. In some apps the audio will split out as a separate layer and sit underneath the video layer. Most timelines work by layering clips and effects on top of, or underneath, one another – like bricks in a wall. Your interview or presentation will sit on the first – or master – layer, and any supplementary footage will sit on the layer above or below. Layers can also be referred to as 'tracks' in some editing apps. If your chosen editing app does not allow 'multitrack editing', it will not be suitable for editing your storyboard videos (all the apps we have suggested allow multitrack editing).

The timeline also has a **playhead**, which is a vertical marker that can be moved forwards and backwards along the timeline. When you click play in the viewer, the footage on the timeline will play from wherever the playhead is positioned. When you add a clip from the media browser to the timeline, it will insert wherever the playhead is positioned.

TOOLS/ACTIONS

The timeline has several tools that enable precise editing. These include:

- **Split/Trim** – sometimes shown as scissors or a razor blade. Use this to trim clips to their desired length.
- **Crop** – sometimes shown as a magnifying glass or two overlapping right angles. Use this to crop into an area of the clip to make it bigger. Do this by pinching the screen then repositioning the image within the viewer window.
- **Undo** – sometimes shown as an arrow curving backwards. Use this to undo an edit you're not happy with.
- **Speed** – sometimes shown as a speedometer or a hare and tortoise – use this to slow down or speed up a clip.
- **Rotate** – sometimes shown as a circular arrow – a useful tool for straightening footage, if it has been filmed slanted. This will create gaps around the frame so you'll also need

to crop in to remove the gaps.

- **Audio editor** – sometimes shown as a speaker or a musical note – use this to control the volume of your clips.
- **Zoom/Magnify** – most timelines have a zoom or magnifying tool that allows you to take a closer look at your clips for precise editing. To zoom, pinch in or out on the timeline.

TRANSITIONS

A transition refers to how one clip ends and the next begins. Most video editors provide a selection of transitions, the most common being dissolve, slide, wipe and fade. We will explain how to use transitions in Chapter 20.

EFFECTS, OVERLAYS, FILTERS & THEMES

Some editing programmes have pre-installed effects that can be dropped onto clips. An effect is any action that alters or distorts the image in some way, such as blur or mosaic. An overlay is an effect that is laid over the image such as a light flare or a picture frame. A filter is an effect that alters the look and colour of the image, such as vintage or black & white. A theme is a set of effects including titles, text, transitions and filters that give your video an overall style. In some apps, the effect can be dropped directly onto a clip, whilst in others it will sit on its own layer on the timeline.

TEXT/TITLES

All editing apps allow you to add text to your videos. You might want to add a title, name captions, information or contact details. Some programmes provide only simple text with a limited choice of fonts and positions, while others have a bigger selection of stylised text options. In most programmes, the text function is accessed by tapping the letter 'T'. In some programmes the text can be dropped directly onto a clip, whilst in others it will sit on its own layer on the timeline.

For further information, visit the Resources section of our website where you'll find further guidance about the individual elements of an editing interface. Book a place on one of our workshops to learn more about video editing – www.myovdo.com/workshops.

18

THE BASIC PRINCIPLES OF VIDEO EDITING

In this chapter we're looking at the basic principles of video editing, which apply regardless of what editing app you're using. It may help you to print out the video storyboard and follow it as you edit. The guiding principle of video editing is: structure first, then embellishments. What does this mean? It means assemble your master clips (interview or presentation) in the right order before adding supplementary footage, transitions, effects or text (we'll show you how to do that in the following chapters).

HOW TO BUILD A SEQUENCE

Building a sequence starts with learning how to trim. In every clip you will have extraneous footage around the dialogue or action that needs to be removed. There are several ways to trim a clip:

1. Start by moving your first clip (Step 1 from your storyboard) from the media browser to the timeline by tapping the clip, then tapping the plus symbol (in some apps the clip will jump to the timeline with a single tap). Magnify the clip by pinching the screen – you will then be able to trim it more precisely.

2. To trim the beginning and end of a clip, tap it to reveal brackets around the clip. Drag the first bracket forwards to the point you would like your clip to start, then drag the end bracket backwards to the point you would like your clip to end. By dragging the brackets you are automatically changing the length of the clip and discarding extraneous footage.

3. To split a clip part way through, drag the timeline forwards or backwards until the playhead is positioned at the point in the clip you would like it to split. Tap on the clip then select the scissors icon or 'Split'. Your clip will become two separate clips; delete the clip you don't need by tapping it and selecting the dustbin icon.

4. You can then trim the remaining clip more precisely, if required, by dragging the brackets as described in point 2.

5. Position the playhead at the end

of the preceding clip, then locate your second clip (Step 2 from your storyboard) in the media browser. Add the clip to the timeline as described above. Remember, the new clip will move to wherever the playhead is positioned, even if it's in the middle of the preceding clip. Don't worry if this happens – just select 'Undo', reposition the playhead then drop the new clip onto the timeline.

6. Trim the new clip as described above. Continue the process of adding and trimming clips until you have built the structure of your video.

7. Review the sequence by moving the playhead to the beginning of the first clip and tapping play. Check that your clips have been added in the correct order and that the sequence flows smoothly. If necessary, go back to individual clips to further trim or extend them as required.

NOTE: when you trim clips you are removing footage only from the timeline, not from the entire device. If you decide to undo a trim action or replace a clip you had previously deleted, you can still access it from your media browser.

CHANGING THE ORDER OF CLIPS

Once you've reviewed the sequence you may decide to change the order of some of the clips. To do this, simply tap and hold the clip until it jumps out of position, then drag it backwards or forwards to its new position between the other clips. When you let go the clip will land in place, nudging the surrounding clips out of the way to make space.

CHANGING THE SOUND LEVEL OR VOLUME OF CLIPS

Once your clips are on the timeline you can increase or decrease the volume of individual clips as required. Highlight the clip by tapping it, then select the speaker icon which will reveal a volume slider. Slide it up or down to reach the desired volume. Your app may also provide a fade in/out function, which can be applied to the beginning and end of clips or sequences to prevent the audio from starting or ending abruptly.

Repeat this process of adding clips to the timeline, then trimming and repositioning them to build the structure of your video sequence.

19

ADDING SUPPLEMENTARY FOOTAGE

Once you have added your master clips (interview or presentation) to the timeline to create the structure of your video, you can then add supplementary footage. Supplementary footage provides interest to your video and it can also be used to cover joins between the master clips underneath. What the viewer sees and hears must have some correlation, so make sure the supplementary clips are relevant to what's being spoken about in the dialogue otherwise you may confuse or mislead the viewer. There is no definite rule for how long a supplementary clip should appear on screen – long enough for the viewer to understand the context, but not too long that it becomes boring or irrelevant.

The method of adding supplementary footage will vary between apps. Let's look at how it's done in the two recommended apps:

iMOVIE*

1. Move the playhead to the point at which you'd like the supplementary clip to begin.
2. Highlight the supplementary clip in the media browser, then tap the three horizontal dots in the dialogue box. This will take you to a second dialogue box containing various symbols. Tap the overlay symbol (a solid box overlapping a dotted box). The clip will jump to the timeline on a layer above the existing clips.
3. Trim or reposition the clip as described in the previous chapter.
4. You'll notice the clip displays a muted speaker, but if you do wish to introduce a low volume of background noise for atmosphere, highlight the clip then tap the volume icon and slide the volume slider to the desired volume.

KINEMASTER*

1. Move the playhead to the point at which you'd like the supplementary clip to begin.
2. Tap 'Layer', then tap the 'Media' icon.
3. Tap the 'Camera' folder then select the supplementary clip. It will jump to the timeline and sit on a layer

underneath the existing clips.

4. The clip will appear in a window smaller than the frame of the viewing window, so hold your finger on the bottom right hand corner of the supplementary clip and stretch it to fit the window.

5. Trim or reposition the clip as described in the previous chapter.

6. The volume does not automatically mute, so highlight the clip, tap the speaker icon and turn the volume low or to zero, as preferred.

* When these apps are updated by the developer, we cannot guarantee these methods will still apply. Check with them directly for operating instructions. If you are using an alternative editing app, consult the app's instructions and tutorials to learn how to add supplementary footage.

ADDING STILL IMAGES

You may wish to add still images or photographs to your video instead of, or as well as, supplementary footage. Different editing applications process still images in different ways. Kinemaster, for example, treats a still image in exactly the same way as a video clip, so it can be added to the timeline as a master clip or supplementary clip using the methods described. In iMovie, however, still images can only be added to the timeline as master clips, not as supplementary clips.

The solution to this is simple: change your still images into video clips. Here's how:

1. In iMovie, start a new movie project.

2. Add your required still image to the timeline as described in Chapter 18.

3. Tap on the image on the timeline and stretch it to your desired length.

4. iMovie automatically adds a movement effect to still images, called the 'Ken Burns effect'. Tap on the clip to reveal the effect controls in the viewer window, where you can either disable the effect or change the start/end position of the movement.

5. If you would like to use more than one still image in your video, add them to the timeline, stretch them and change the effect preferences as described above. IMovie will automatically place a 'dissolve' transition between each clip. Disable the transition by tapping the square between the clips and selecting 'none' (represented by a vertical line).

6. When you have finished, select 'Done', then rename the video by tapping on 'My Movie' and changing it to 'Still Image Sequence', for example.

7. Select the share icon (represented by a square with an upwards-pointing arrow at the top) then select 'Save Video'. The image sequence will be saved to your device's photo gallery as a video clip.

8. When you return to your master video project, you can add the still image sequence as a supplementary clip, as described above. If you have added more than one image to the sequence, simply split the clip to extract the individual images and position them on your timeline as required.

To watch a video of this process, visit the Resources section of our website – www.myovdo.com.

REVIEW YOUR SEQUENCE

Once you have added your supplementary clips to the timeline, watch the video from the beginning. Check that the supplementary clips correspond to the dialogue, that they remain on screen for a comfortable amount of time, and that their audio (if you're using it) sits comfortably in the background without obscuring the dialogue. Make changes as required then review the video again. In the next chapter we'll show you how to embellish your video with effects and text.

If you would like further guidance on any aspects of video editing, visit www.myovdo.com/shop to book a consultation.

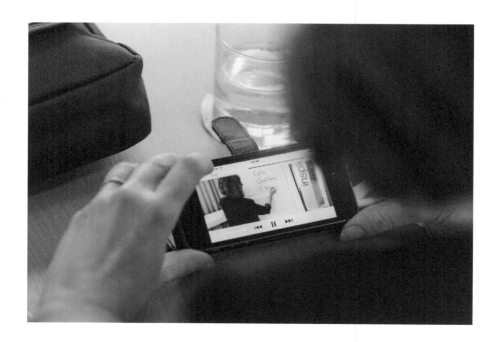

HOW TO ADD EFFECTS AND TEXT

In this chapter we're looking at how to embellish your videos by adding effects and text. Both should be used sparingly to enhance the viewing experience; overuse can bewilder the viewer.

EFFECTS

Visual effects include filters, themes and transitions. Let's look in more detail.

Filters

Filters are effects that alter the entire clip by changing the colours, clarity or movement. There are two types of filters: corrective and stylistic. Corrective filters help you to improve the image or remedy any 'mistakes' made during filming such as brightness, contrast or colour balance. Stylistic filters are used to establish a certain look and feel such as vintage, sunny day or black and white. Most editing apps contain a variety of filters to help you achieve the desired effect. They can usually be accessed through an 'Effects' or 'Filters' icon. You can also change the speed of a clip to create a slow motion or fast forward effect using the speedometer icon.

Themes

Some apps contain a choice of themes, which are collections of effects, transitions, and captions that can be applied to your entire video to give it an overall style. Examples of themes include 'travel', 'news', 'playful' and 'modern'. If you decide to apply a theme, make sure it's appropriate for the type of video you're making. Where available, themes are usually accessed through the app's Settings menu, or can be selected when you start a project.

Transitions

A transition refers to how one clip ends and the next begins. The simplest transition is called a **cut**, where one clip simply follows another. Cuts are common in video editing and denote continuity from one scene to another. However, most apps contain several transition effects, which are used to suggest certain messages to the viewer. A **cross dissolve** is where one clip gradually merges into the next, evoking a sense of nostalgia or the passage of time. A **slide** is where one clip moves in from the left, right, top or bottom, pushing the preceding clip out of frame. Slides are suited to fast-paced videos, or when you want to denote a shift in setting, subject or circumstances. A **fade** is where one clip gradually fades out to black before fading into the next clip. Fades are commonly used to signify the end of one thing and the beginning of another, such as an event or a day.

When a transition is applied, the two clips essentially overlap each other for the duration of the transition. This is one reason why it's important to leave editing handles during filming. In some apps the transition affects the audio as well, so if you don't leave handles at either side of your dialogue, the words will overlap as well as the footage. Transition effects should be used sparingly to avoid distracting the viewer.

The method of applying a transition will vary from app to app. In some, a small square icon will appear between each clip as you add clips to the timeline. Simply tap the icon to reveal the choice of transitions. In other apps there will be a transitions option which, when selected, will reveal the choice of transitions. When a transition is selected, it will jump to the timeline between two clips.

TEXT

Text can be added to a video to let the viewer know what it is about and to provide additional information not mentioned in the dialogue or shown within the footage. To add text, select the 'T' icon. Here are some things to consider when adding text:

Purpose

There are several reasons to add text to videos: add the **title** of the video at the beginning, add **name captions** of people appearing in the video, add additional **information** or **subtitles** throughout and add **contact details** at the end.

Font, Size And Colour

Ideally, the font, size and colour of the text will suit the style of the video. You may also want it to correspond with your company branding. Be aware that some viewers may be watching your video on a smartphone, so the text must be visible even on a small screen. Certain fonts and colours can be difficult to read, especially positioned against high contrast backgrounds.

Position

In some editing apps, the text is fixed in certain positions – usually central or lower left/right. Central text is usually used for titles whilst lower text is used for name captions. Other apps give you more flexibility over positioning. Just remember not to place text too close to the edges of the frame, obscure any people or important action. If you are making a square video, position the text in the area that won't be removed during the cropping stage.

Amount

Text should be used sparingly. Too much text can be offputting for your viewer, especially if they're not given enough time to read it. The exception to this is when adding subtitles (videos that play muted in social media news feeds should always display subtitles). To learn more about the importance of using subtitles in videos and how to do it, visit www.myovdo. com/advanced.

TIP: Some mobile editing apps provide preset text styles which cannot be customised. For more control over fonts, colour, size and positioning of text, consider adding text afterwards using a separate 'text on video' app (search the App or Play Store). Simply edit your video without text, save it to your picture gallery, download your preferred text app, open your video in the app, add text, then save to your gallery again ready to upload to social media.

21

RECORDING A VOICE-OVER

In this chapter we're looking at how to record a voice-over and add supplementary footage. Voice-over is narration that is not accompanied by footage of the person speaking. The storyboard videos can all be made with voice-over instead of an interview or presentation. Most video editing apps have a voice-over recording function, usually represented by a microphone symbol. Follow these steps to make a voice-over video.

1. Write your voice-over script by following a storyboard, then create a list of footage to shoot.

2. Shoot your footage as described in Chapter 15.

3. Open your video editing app, create a new project and locate your footage in the media browser.

4. Some editing apps will not allow you to record a voice-over until you have placed footage on the timeline. If this is the case, add your clips to the timeline in the order stated in the storyboard. It doesn't matter if they're not placed accurately at this stage – you can edit more precisely once your voice-over is on the timeline. If your programme allows you to record a voice-over first, do so.

5. Attach your tie-clip mic into the head-phone socket of your device and find a quiet location with no echo. A small room with soft furnishings is ideal.

6. Launch the voice recorder by tapping the microphone symbol. Some programmes will display an audio meter for checking the sound level. This may look like a vertical or horizontal bar that shows a coloured light when it registers sound. A green light signifies a decent level, an orange light means it's heading towards danger, and a red light means it's too loud. Keep the level in the green range. If it's too loud, move your microphone further away from your mouth.

7. Position the playhead to where you would like the audio clip to appear on the timeline, then start recording. Record each section of the script as a separate clip, deleting the bad takes as you go.

8. When you have finished recording, trim the audio clips if necessary (as described in Chapter 18).

9. Position the corresponding video clips accurately on the timeline by moving and trimming them as described in Chapter 18.

10. Mute, or reduce the volume of, the footage by highlighting the clips, tapping the speaker icon then sliding the volume slider to the desired volume. The voice-over should be clearly audible above any background sound.

Once you have edited your video as described above, add text and effects as desired. You may also want to add music and we'll show you how to do this in the next chapter.

22

ADDING BACKGROUND MUSIC

In this chapter we're going to show you how to add background music to your videos. Adding the right music can draw together the themes of your video, making it feel complete. Music can also be used to add pace and to influence your viewers' emotions.

WHAT MUSIC CAN YOU USE?

Some editing apps provide a limited selection of pre-installed music that you can use as you please. There are some websites offering free background music for videos. Check the licensing conditions of these tracks carefully before you use them, as they may only be free for a limited time, or the producer may require a written credit in your video.

Free music should not be confused with 'royalty free': tracks for which you pay a one-off fee, but don't then have to pay a royalty every time the track is played. There are many royalty free music libraries offering thousands of tracks of various moods and genres.

BE AWARE: you cannot use commercial music in your videos – if you do you are breaching copyright laws and risk having your video blocked from social media channels. Commercial music is any track that has been written, performed and recorded for commercial gain. If you weren't the writer, performer or producer of the track, the copyright belongs to someone else so you can't legally use it.

HOW TO ADD MUSIC TO YOUR VIDEOS

1. If you have sourced music online, download it and save it to your device's music folder.
2. Open the editing app and select the project to which you want to add music.
3. In the media browser, locate the music track you wish to use.
4. Position the playhead at the point on the timeline you want the track to start – usually at the very beginning of the video sequence.
5. Highlight the track in the media browser and tap the plus button (or tap the track) to add it to the timeline.
6. If the track is longer than your video sequence, trim it as described in Chapter 18 (unless the app has automatically trimmed it). If the track

is shorter than your edited sequence, repeat the track and trim it to length.

7. Add a fade-in to the beginning of the track and a fade-out at the end.
8. Reduce the overall volume of the track until it sits comfortably in the background without obscuring any dialogue.

For an advanced module in how to make a music video, visit www.myovdo.com/advanced.

23

REVIEWING AND SAVING YOUR VIDEO

You've worked through the editing section and now have a video you're ready to share with your target audience. Before you do, review it one last time and save it to your cloud storage. Here's how:

REVIEWING YOUR VIDEO

Watch the video from the beginning to check that it flows smoothly, that the supplementary clips correspond with the dialogue, that the text is spelt correctly and that the sound is clearly audible. If not, go back into the editing app and make these final tweaks.

SAVING YOUR VIDEO

Once you're happy with your video, save it to your picture gallery, then to your cloud storage. Here's how:

1. Some apps – especially if they are free with in-app purchases – will add a brand watermark to the end of the video. To remove this you'll need to upgrade to an inexpensive plan, which we recommend you do.

2. Open the video in your editing app, select 'Share' (represented either as a square with an arrow, or three dots connected by two lines) then select 'Save to Gallery' or 'Save to Pictures'. The video will be copied into your device's image gallery.

3. If you have already set your device to automatically back up photos and videos to the cloud, your video will be backed up from the gallery as soon as your device has a wifi connection.

4. If you'd prefer to override this and upload manually, select the video from the gallery, select 'Share', then select your cloud storage option. Alternatively, load the cloud storage app and upload the video from within the app.

5. Check that the video has completely copied to the gallery and uploaded to the cloud before deleting any files. We recommend leaving the project in the editing app and leaving all associated footage in the gallery until you have uploaded the video to all desired social media channels. Why? Because you may need to re-edit

the video to make it compatible with specific social media channels, such as making your video square or adding subtitles for Facebook. We'll explain this in more detail in the next section of the book.

6. If you have made a video specifically for the square viewing windows of some social media channels, go into your app store and download a video cropping app – there are plenty of free options. Open the app then locate the video from the gallery. Select 'Square', then position the square frame over the exact part of the video you want to keep. Select 'Crop' or tap the tick icon. The video should automatically save to your gallery.

In the uploading section we'll show you how to upload your video to your chosen social media channels, tactics for maximising views and how to analyse the success of each video. For further guidance on any aspect of editing your video, visit www.myovdo.com/shop to book a one to one consultation. For more information on the latest video marketing trends and insights follow our blog and sign up to our newsletter at www.myovdo.com or attend one of our workshops.

You've filmed and edited your video; the next step is to share it with your target audience. In this section we'll guide you through the process of setting up social media channels, uploading your videos and optimising them to increase their chances of being found. Then we'll look at how to analyse the success of your videos... and how to improve them for next time.

24

HOW TO SET UP SOCIAL MEDIA CHANNELS

In this chapter we're looking at how to set up social media channels. Social media channels include YouTube, Facebook, Twitter, Instagram, Pinterest, LinkedIn, and many hundreds more. So, what channels do you need to set up? Whichever channels your target audience uses – you may have made a note of this when you created your viewer profile in Chapter 3.

TIP: If you intend to use your videos on your website as well as social media, we recommend setting up a YouTube account regardless of whether your target audience uses it. We'll explain more about this in Chapter 27.

Set up your accounts through a computer rather than a mobile device, as you'll have more control over the channel settings. There are two stages to setting up a channel: creating an account and personalisation. To create an account, follow the instructions of the individual channels. The personalisation stage will vary from channel to channel, but here are the options they may share in common:

PROFILE PHOTO/ICON

If your channel represents you as an individual, use an image of yourself. Use a good quality photo that captures a true likeness. Use a plain background and make sure the image is in focus and well lit. If your channel represents a business, you may prefer to use your logo instead. Refer to individual channels for optimum file sizes.

HEADER IMAGE

At the top of most channel pages you'll find a place holder for a header image. Think of this as a billboard to promote your offering. The advice is usually to change this image periodically to maintain interest. You might use an image of a product, an image of customers using your product or service, your mission statement or brand values, or details about an offer, campaign or competition. Again, refer to individual channels for optimum file sizes.

CHANNEL TITLE

Use your company name, although you

may also want to consider including keywords that your target audience commonly use to find the services you offer.

DESCRIPTION/ OVERVIEW

Describe what your channel is about and the type of content you'll be sharing. Include your most important information first, as this is what viewers will see in search results. Here are some content suggestions: the nature of your business, product or service; the sector in which you operate; the benefits of using your product or service; how often you'll be posting new content; A call to action for viewers to subscribe/ like/ comment/ share; links to your website and other social media channels.

THEME & LAYOUT

Some channels allow you to pick from a selection of themes and layouts, which include different coloured backgrounds and fonts. Choose a theme and layout that best suits the nature of your business or offering, and make it consistent across your social media channels.

ABOUT/ INFORMATION

Some channels allow you to add operational details such as where your business is located, opening times and contact information. You may also be able to add a map that automatically links to a satellite navigation system.

CALL TO ACTION

Facebook has added a Call To Action button to its business pages. This sits at the top of the page on the header image. You can choose from a number of calls to action such as 'sign up', 'watch video', 'contact us' or 'shop now'.

OTHER

Individual channels may provide personalisation options not mentioned above. If they do, use them. Personalisation increases the chances of your target viewer finding your channels.

25

HOW TO UPLOAD VIDEOS TO SOCIAL MEDIA

In this chapter we're looking at how to upload your videos to different social media channels from your mobile device. Here's how:

1. If you have set up your channels on a computer, the first thing you'll need to do is install the apps of all relevant channels to your mobile device. Go to your app store and search for the individual channels then tap 'Install'. Wait until they have installed, then login to the apps using the same login details you defined when setting up the channels. There are two ways to upload videos...

2a. The first method is to open your device's gallery and locate the video you'd like to upload. Tap the video to select it, then tap 'Share'. If you have successfully downloaded and logged in to the social media apps, they should appear as sharing options. Select the channel to which you'd like to upload your video and wait until it uploads.

2b. The second method is to do it from within the apps themselves. Open the app then select 'Upload' or tap the camera icon. You will then be taken to your device's gallery, from where you can select the video you want to upload.

3. Repeat the process to upload videos to other channels.

LINKING VIDEOS FROM A HOST CHANNEL

There is, however, an exception. If you're using method 2a and the app's icon doesn't appear as a sharing option, this means the channel does not support 'native' video. Native means a channel can host video on its own server. Non-native means a video must be linked from a host channel such as YouTube. Here's how to link video from a host channel:

1. Set up a host channel such as YouTube (see Chapter 24), then upload a video following one of the methods above.

2. Once the video has uploaded, tap on it then tap the 'Share' icon – this is represented as a right-facing arrow. You then have two options...

3a. The first option is to select the app for the channel to which you'd like to post the video, then follow the instructions.

3b. For the second option, select 'Copy Link' on a mobile device – or copy the URL on a computer – then navigate out of YouTube and open the channel app to which you'd like to post the video. Find the location in which you'd like to paste the link, such as a new update or post. Tap and hold in the location until a 'paste' message appears – select it. The video link will appear along with a thumbnail image from the video.

4. Repeat the process to share video links to other non-native channels.

TIP: You may need to make different versions of the same video for different channels. For example, square video is better than 16:9 video for Instagram and we recommend that Facebook videos contain subtitles because they play without audio in the news feed. To learn more about subtitling, visit www.myovdo. com/advanced.

26

HOW TO OPTIMISE VIDEOS TO HELP VIEWERS FIND THEM

In this chapter we're looking at how to change the settings of your video once it has been uploaded to social media. Settings include the video's title, description and thumbnail image. Why would you want to change these settings? Quite simply, to help your viewers find your videos more easily. This process is called 'optimisation'. Every channel will have its own unique optimisation methods, but they also have some in common. Here's what to look for:

TITLES & HEADINGS

The title of your video is how viewers find it, so it's important to word it with consideration. Think about the **search terms** they might use to find the information you are offering, and include them in the title (popular search terms include 'how to', 'what is', review, 'top 10' and 'best way to'). Keep it **short**; stick to 50 characters or less so the whole title appears in search results. Your title must **accurately** reflect the video content, not mislead the viewer.

DESCRIPTION

The description is an opportunity to explain the contents of your video. You may wish to include the following information: repeat the **title** of the video to reiterate the search terms; provide a detailed **synopsis**, including why you made it and the **benefits** viewers will gain from watching it; include **links** to your website, other videos and other social media channels; also include links to the websites of other products, services, people or brands mentioned in the video; add a **call to action**, either repeating the CTA in the video or something else such as like, share or subscribe; include **tags** – words relevant to your video.

TAGS

As well as including tags in the description, the video settings may also include a tags box. Use as many tags as you think is necessary and relevant, separating each tag with a comma.

THUMBNAIL IMAGE

This is a still image that represents your video when it appears on social media channels and in search results, almost like a book cover. Most channels will randomly select an image, but it may not be the best one to 'sell' your video content. The channel may allow you to choose from a selection of randomly generated images. If so, choose the one you think represents your video in its best light. If you'd like to learn how to make a custom thumbnail image, visit www.myovdo.com/advanced.

CASE STUDY

Here's a hypothetical case study based on our Overview storyboard. The video has been made by NuSmile Dental Practice based in Basingstoke to introduce their teeth whitening service to a new audience.

Title: Affordable Teeth Whitening Basingstoke NuSmile Dentist

Overview/ Description: Are you looking for affordable teeth whitening in Basingstoke? NuSmile Dental Practice has the solution. We have developed an affordable payment plan to make teeth whitening accessible for everyone. In this video we show you an overview of our teeth whitening service – before and after – and explain the payment options. After watching this video you will see how easy and accessible teeth whitening can be. Give your confidence a boost – contact NuSmile Dental Practice today to make your appointment.
www.nusmiledentist.co/whitening
www.facebook.com/nusmiledentist
Call to make your appointment: 01234 567890

Tags: teeth whitening, affordable teeth whitening, dentist, nusmile dentist, nusmile dental practice, dentist basingstoke, teeth whitening basingstoke, youtube, basingstoke, teeth, smile, nusmile, new smile, affordable dentist

27

HOW TO ADD VIDEOS TO YOUR WEBSITE

In this chapter we're looking briefly at how to add videos to your website. The five video storyboards have been specially created with your website in mind; when you've made these videos you can strategically position them on different pages of your website to maximise visitor engagement.

The first step towards adding videos to your website is to upload them to a host channel such as YouTube, as described in Chapter 25. Hosting on a social media channel instead of your website means the video isn't taking up valuable space on your own website's server, slowing down the loading speed of each page. Once you've uploaded the video to the host site, change the settings to 'Public' and 'Allow Embedding'. The next step depends on how your website was built.

If it was created by a developer and he or she continues to maintain your site, simply copy the video's YouTube link, paste it into an email and send it to your developer, letting him or her know where on the site you would like the video to be positioned.

If you built your own website, you will have access to the site's control panel via a login screen. Copy the YouTube link and paste it into the relevant area of the site builder. We recommend you do this on a computer not a mobile device. Save any changes then refresh the website in your browser to see the video.

28

HOW TO MEASURE THE SUCCESS OF YOUR VIDEOS

In this final chapter we're looking at how to measure the success of your videos: whether or not your videos achieved what you set out to achieve. Video, like any other form of marketing, must be tested over a period of time. As we have discussed, there are ways throughout the video making process to maximise success, but there is no certainty until you start to share your videos with an audience.

Many channels provide detailed data on visitor numbers and behaviour. How do you access this data? Login to your social media accounts and look for the words 'Analytics', 'Insights' or 'Stats'. As a guide, here are the indicators of success to look out for:

VIDEO VIEWS

This is the number of views your video has gained. See the diagram in the resources section of the website to find out what counts as a 'view' on different platforms. Quantity of views doesn't always translate into quality, unless you have monetised your video with the objective of getting as many views as possible. If your objective was to achieve more sales, look at the number of views in relation to sales to see if you can find a correlation. If the number of views is disappointing, it might be because your target audience is using different platforms, or that your keywords don't match your target audience's search terms.

QUALITY OF VIEWERS

Some platforms will provide a breakdown of views into categories such as age, gender, geographical location and the source of the view (click-throughs from other channels or a website). These statistics can be useful for finding out whether your video is reaching your target audience. If not, consider whether you are using the right keywords in your video settings, or whether the content might be unappealing. If your video is reaching its target audience, are your viewers engaging with your video in the ways you'd expected and are your objectives being met?

AUDIENCE RETENTION

This shows how much of a video your viewers are watching. If they are consistently dropping off after a period of time, it might be because your video is too long, or that the content isn't relevant. Try shortening existing videos and making subsequent videos shorter. If drop-off is due to irrelevancy, it might be as a result of having too many messages in one video, or that the content or style doesn't appeal to your target audience.

ENGAGEMENT

Statistics can only tell you so much about a video's success. For more qualitative insights look at viewer engagement: likes, shares, comments, followers and subscribers. Simply asking your viewers to engage does not guarantee they will, especially if they feel indifferent about your content. Likes, share, follows and subscriptions usually indicate that you have reached your target audience and they are interested in your messages. Comments – both positive and negative – are useful because they provide genuine insights into what's working and what isn't. Use this feedback to improve your future videos.

VIEWING DEVICES

Some platforms will provide percentage figures of what devices people are using to view your videos. This can help you hone your content to optimise the viewing experience. For example, if most views are coming from mobile, you might assume your viewers are 'on the go' rather than static at a desk. They may not have a lot of time, so keep your videos short. They may be in noisy environments, so add captions and text. They are viewing on a small screen, so ensure your clips and text are clear and easy to read. CTA's should be easy to action on the go from a mobile.

CALL TO ACTION

Have you included a call to action in your video, and if so, how are you measuring its success? If you've asked viewers to like, share, comment or subscribe, are they doing so? If you've asked them to contact you, download a report or provide feedback, how are you maximising this engagement – perhaps by implementing a follow-up procedure? If your videos are getting views but no engagement, consider changing your call to action, your message, the style of your videos, or posting them on different platforms.

ASK FOR FEEDBACK

Finally, consider sending your videos to a select group of specific people in your target market and asking them for feedback. Create a series of questions to ask after they have viewed – either in person or through a survey.

EXPERIMENT...

Analysing video viewing data is crucial to help you understand what videos work best. The key is to experiment; if your first few videos don't achieve your desired results, look at the data, make some changes and try again. It may take a while but with perseverance you will eventually learn what types of videos are most effective for your target audiences.

Why not share your video making experiences with the rest of the MYOVDO community? Join the Facebook group through www.facebook.com/myovdoforum and sign up to our newsletter at www.myovdo.com to find out more about our webinars with experts in video making and marketing.

PRODUCTION _____

DIRECTOR _____

CAMERA _____

DATE	SCENE	TAKE

CONCLUSION

As you have hopefully seen by reading this handbook, it is possible for someone with no prior knowledge or experience of making videos to plan, shoot, edit and upload simple yet high quality promotional videos using just one device. With this book, our objective is to provide foundation skills that set you on a journey of self empowerment – enabling you to use the technology you may already own to grow your business through targeted videos.

Our five unique storyboards will help you devise a simple, yet effective video communications plan, guiding your viewers along a journey from awareness to engagement. The storyboards can be adapted to suit any type of business or organisation, and the steps can be tailored to your message and objectives. When you're ready to progress, you'll find storyboards for many other types of videos at www.myovdo.com/storyboards, which can be purchased as required.

This handbook is designed to provide the foundation skills for video making; only when you put the theory into practice will the real learning begin. Make Your Own

Video Training Academy offers continued support in several ways: book on to one of our practical workshops where our expert trainers will guide you through the process of making a video from start to finish (www.myovdo.com/workshops); book a one-to-one consultation to talk through any aspect of video making (www.myovdo.com/shop); join our social media communities for peer discussions as well as input from trainers; and sign up to our newsletter for news of current trends in video production. You can also purchase advanced video modules to learn new skills and techniques as you progress along your video making journey. You'll find these at www.myovdo.com/advanced.

For additional support, we have created a set of resource materials to help consolidate your learning as you progress through the Handbook and workshop. The resources are free for you to access through our website. Simply visit www.myovdo.com/resources and register with your email address and the following code: MYOHBF. You will then receive an email containing a password so you can login to access the resources.

We also offer full service video production

if you have a video project beyond the scope of the skills we're sharing through Make Your Own Video Training Academy. Whilst there are many types of videos you can make easily by yourself, sometimes you may need professional expertise, experienced crew and specialist equipment to produce a video that meets your objectives. Visit www.myovdo.com/videoproduction to find out more.

Our mission is to help you succeed as a video maker. The best advice we can give you now? **Put this book down and start shooting!**

JOIN THE MYOVDO COMMUNITY

Visit our website and signup to our newsletter: www.myovdo.com

Access the resources: www.myovdo.com/resources
and register with your email address and code MYOHBF

Purchase equipment: www.myovdo.com/shop

Book your place on a workshop: www.myovdo.com/workshops

Purchase more Storyboards: www.myovdo.com/storyboards

See our advanced courses: www.myovdo.com/advanced

Join the Facebook forum: www.facebook.com/groups/myovdoforum

Ask us about professional video production: info@myovdo.com

Send us an email: info@myovdo.com

Shout about Make Your
Own Video Training
Academy and share
your videos:

#MYOVDO

GLOSSARY

A

Action – any movement or activity that takes place in front of the camera, and the command called by the video director for the person in front of the camera to start their activity.

Aeroplane mode – a setting on your mobile device that disables wifi and telephone connectivity.

Android – the operating system for mobile devices devised and run by Google. Other operating systems include iOS (Apple) and Windows (Microsoft).

Aperture – the iris of a camera lens that controls the amount of light reaching the sensor by opening or closing. *See also* Sensor.

Application or **App** – a programme or piece of software with a defined purpose, designed to run on smart devices such as smartphones and tablets.

Aspect ratio – the ratio of the width to the height of a video screen, represented as two numbers separated by a colon. The first number represents the width and the second number represents the height. 'Widescreen' has an aspect ratio of 16:9. Square screens have an aspect ration of 1:1.

Audience – the people watching your videos. Your target audience may be different for each video you make; understanding their behaviour and characteristics will enable you to produce audience specific content.

Audio – the sound captured in your video.

This includes people talking, background sound, and music.

Audio file – the format in which audio is stored digitally. Common audio formats are .MP3 and .WAV.

Avatar – an icon, image or figure representing a person.

B

Backdrop – items you have strategically positioned to appear in the background of your shot. This might include curtains, banners, pictures, furniture or objects.

Background – anything behind the main focus of action. It could be a backdrop you have specially created, or an existing setting you have deliberately chosen to film in front of.

C

Call To Action (CTA) – a message in your video telling viewers to undertake a specific action such as get in touch, share, like, sign-up, visit the website or donate.

Camera – a device that captures an image or video. In this book we are teaching you how to use the video camera within your mobile device, rather than a dedicated camera. *See also* Filming device, Mobile device.

Camera operator – the person responsible for setting up the filming device and recording the footage. The camera operator may also be the director and the interviewer.

Capacity – the maximum amount of digital information a mobile device can contain. Standard capacities are 16, 32, 64 and 128 gigabytes (GB). *See also* Internal Storage.

Channel – an online portal through which multiple users can communicate. Social Media channels include Facebook, Twitter, LinkedIn and YouTube.

Clip – a piece of video recorded by a camera, also called a shot. A video sequence comprises a number of video clips edited together. *See also* Sequence, Shot.

Closed captions – text displayed on screen that transcribes the dialogue and sounds of a video for the benefit of hearing impaired viewers, or for when a video plays muted. On certain social media channels, closed captions can be turned on and off by the viewer. *See also* Subtitles.

Closed questions – a type of question that would elicit a limited response such as yes, no, or one-word answers. Closed questions are not recommended for video interviews; open questions are preferable. *See also* Open questions.

Cloud editing – editing footage using a web-based editing programme. The footage is stored on a remote server rather than on your own computer, hard drive or storage device. *See also* Editing, Remote server.

Cloud storage – space purchased on a remote server on which to store data. It is accessed through a computer or mobile device with a wifi connection. *See also* Remote server.

Composition – the arrangement of elements, such as people, objects and backgrounds within a video frame. *See also* Frame.

Consent form – a document signed by anyone appearing in your video, confirming that they will not object – either now or in the future – to you using the footage and audio you have captured of them.

Content – specifically, video content. Anything that you have filmed or created and want to include in your video such as interviews, presentations, supplementary footage, text or graphics.

Continuity – keeping every aspect of your filming, such as lighting, clothing, props, action and sound quality consistent from one shot to another.

Contributor – the person you are filming such as an interviewee or presenter, particularly if they have a speaking role (especially providing a particular point of view or specialist knowledge). *See also* Interviewee, Subject.

Cut – the end of one shot and the beginning of another in the editing process. It is also the director's command to stop filming.

D

Delivery mode – the way the information in your video is delivered. In this book we talk about three distinct modes of delivery: interview, presentation and voice-over. *See also* Interview, Presentation, Voice-over.

Diffused lighting – light that has been softened in some way. A common way to diffuse light is to shine it through a membrane such as a voile curtain or a specialist photographic lighting filter.

Director – the person responsible for what

footage is captured. The director has a vision of what they want to achieve, and will tell the people in front of the camera what to do. In a small film crew the director may also be the camera operator, interviewer and editor.

Distort – distorted audio is audio that has been recorded so loud that some of the digital information has been lost.

E

Echo – the noise of sound waves bouncing off surfaces and reflecting back to you. Echo is likely to occur in rooms with hard surfaces. **Echo** can be removed by introducing materials that absorb the sound waves such as carpets, curtains and other soft furnishings.

Editing – the process of assembling different clips of footage to create a single video.

Editing handles – space filmed at the beginning and end of a video clip before and after any action.

Effect – an action in video editing that distorts or alters the image in some way. Filters, overlays and transitions are examples of video effects.

Engagement – interaction following the viewing of a video such as likes, shares and comments on social media channels, increased visitors to a website or increased sales.

Export – moving a video file from a video editing programme to a particular destination, in a particular format.

External microphone – A separate microphone that is plugged into the headphone socket of your camera or filming device, usually capturing clearer audio than the device's internal microphone. *See also* Internal microphone, Tie-clip microphone.

Eyeline – the line of sight of the person in front of the camera. In a presentation video their eyeline will be towards the camera. In an interview video their eyeline will be towards an interviewer positioned at the side of the camera. The eyeline will also be affected by the height of the camera in relation to the height of the person being filmed; unless the camera and eyes are level, the person will either be looking upwards or downwards.

F

File size – when referring to a digital image, the size is usually represented by the number of pixels wide, by the number of pixels high. *See also* Pixel.

Filming device – a tablet or smart device that has an internal camera and video capturing application. *See also* Camera, Mobile device.

Focus – the clarity and sharpness of the video image. Your device's camera is set to focus automatically but there may be occasions when you need to switch to manual focus.

Frame – the area you can see on the screen of your filming device when using the camera. *See also* Framing.

Frames per second (fps) – the number of still images, or frames, comprising every second of video. The European broadcasting standard is 25 frames per second; this means that every second of video is comprised of 25 still images.

Framing – how much of the scene you choose to capture in your frame. You might have a building, some trees and a group of people in front of you, but you might choose to capture only the people. *See also* Rule of framing.

G

Gaffer tape – heavy cotton tape with strong adhesive properties. It can be purchased from most hardware stores and is usually black or silver in colour.

Gigabytes or **GB** – a byte is a unit of data, or information. A gigabyte is one thousand million bytes. 10 minutes of video is approximately 1.5 gigabytes.

Good take – when everything goes well whilst filming, resulting in a useable clip. The opposite is called an outtake. *See also* Outtake.

H

Handles – *see* Editing handles

Hard drive – a physical device on which data is stored.

Headroom – the space in a video frame between the top of the subject's head and the top of the frame. Too much head room and your subject will be too low in the frame. Too little head room and you will be in danger of cropping the top of their head out of the frame if they move during filming.

High Definition (HD) – the level of detail recorded by a camera or displayed on a screen. HD cameras shoot frames of 1920 pixels wide by 1080 pixels deep. *See also* Resolution.

Host site – a video sharing platform such as YouTube. Video is too large to place on a website or send via email so a video must first be uploaded to a host site and linked to websites or emails from the host site. *See also* Channel.

I

Interface – relating specifically to a video editing programme, this is what is visible on a screen when an editing programme is opened. A typical editing interface contains a media browser, a viewer, a timeline and a tool palette. *See also* Media browser, Timeline, Tool Palette, Viewer.

Internal microphone – the microphone built into your camera or filming device. Internal mics capture all sounds without discrimination. When filming someone speaking, it is better to attach an external microphone, which will prioritise voice over background noise. *See also* External microphone.

Internal storage – every mobile device contains an internal storage drive which holds data. Devices commonly hold 16, 32, 64 or 128GB of data. Video takes up a lot of space so it's advisable to delete footage or move it to an external or cloud storage drive to make room for new footage. *See also* Capacity.

Interview – a filming method or mode of delivering information where a person is positioned in front of the camera answering questions asked by an interviewer positioned to the side of the camera. During filming, the interviewee looks at the interviewer, not at the camera.

Interviewee – the person being filmed during an interview.

Interviewer – the person asking the questions during an interview.

iOS – the mobile operating system devised and developed by Apple Inc. Other operating systems include Android (Google) and Windows (Microsoft).

J

Jack plug – a cylindrical connector commonly found on the end of headphone wires and also on microphones specifically used with mobile devices. The jack plug fits into the headphone socket of a mobile device. *See also* TRS, TRRS.

Jump cut – in a video, a jump cut is when one clip cuts abruptly to the next, giving the impression that the footage has jumped. This style is commonly used in vlogs. *See also* Vlog

K

Keywords (*see also* Search terms) – words and phrases commonly used in online searches.

L

Landing page – A specific web page that a visitor lands on when they visit a website. This can be a stand alone page, separate from the website, that a visitor is directed towards if they have entered certain keywords or search criteria. It is used as a way of directing visitors to highly relevant web content.

Lens – this is the 'eye' of the camera. Your mobile device (or filming device) has two lenses – one on the front and one on the back. It is a small circle of glass that allows light through and on to a sensor behind.

Level – this refers to the volume of audio you are recording. If your level is set too high there's a danger your sound will distort, which means some of the digital information has been lost.

Lighting – the deliberate use of light to achieve a desired visual effect. This includes the use of natural daylight as well as artificial light from lamps and light fixtures.

Link – a link is the address of a particular web page or piece of online content such as a video. When a video is uploaded to a social media platform, it is assigned a specific address (or link) which can be copied and pasted in other online locations, linking the viewer back to the original location.

Location – the place where your filming takes place. This could be a space in your home or office, or somewhere you have hired especially to film your video. *See also* Backdrop, Background.

Lower third – the term given to text in a video that appears in the lower part of the screen, usually to the left or the right. Commonly, this is a name caption of the person appearing in the video but it could also be facts, instructions or subtitles. *See also* Name caption, Rule of thirds, Subtitles.

M

Marker – a small piece of masking tape on the floor indicating where your subject should be positioned in front of the camera.

Media browser – The area of a video editing interface from where the source footage is accessed. *See also* Editing, Interface, Source footage.

Microphone – a device for recording audio. Abbreviated as 'mic'. *See also* External microphone, Internal microphone.

Microphone extension cable – a cable to extend the length of a microphone cable. Using an extension cable enables you to position your subject further away from the camera.

Mobile device – a smartphone or tablet, usually with wi-fi. In this book we are using mobile devices as the camera, editor and upload vehicle for our videos. *See also* Camera, Filming device.

Monetise, **monetize** – when you monetise a video on YouTube for example, you sign up to a programme allowing advertisers to place adverts on your videos. You earn a share of the revenue generated from views or click-throughs.

Montage video – a video comprising entirely of footage and music (no dialogue).

Mount – a holder that allows you to attach a tablet or smartphone securely to a tripod.

N

Name caption – text in a video that tells the viewer the name and title of the person speaking. It is usually positioned on the lower left or lower right of the screen. *See also* Lower third.

Native video – video uploaded directly to a social media platform rather than linked to it from a host site. *See also* Host site.

News feed – a list of newly published content (including videos) by friends or followers on a social media channel.

O

Off-camera – any action taking place outside of the camera's or filming device's point of view (frame). It will not be captured in your footage because your camera can't see it. For example, if you are filming an interview, you may have an interviewee in front of the camera and an interviewer off-camera.

Online – relating to the internet.

Open questions – the opposite of closed questions. Any question posed to an interviewee that elicits a lengthy response rather than a one word answer. *See also* Closed questions.

Open rate – the number of viewers that choose to open an email or click on a link to view further content.

Optimisation – the act of making online content easy to find and attractive to open, watch, share or engage with in some way. Using keywords in video content, titles and descriptions is a form of optimisation. Providing relevant content for a specific audience is another. *See also* Keywords, Search Engine Optimisation.

Organic – specifically related to search results. When a search engine provides results, there are usually two types of listings: organic and paid. Organic listings appear as a result of relevance to the search terms inputted. Paid results are advertisements paid for by the website owner. *See also* Search Engine Optimisation.

Outtake – when filming, an outtake is a clip you discard because it contains a human or technical error. *See also* Good take.

P

Pan – the smooth movement of a camera from left to right (or vice versa) from a fixed position (like turning your head).

Pixel – Every digital image consists of pixels – tiny squares of colour. The more pixels a camera can shoot, or a screen can display, the higher the image quality. *See also* High definition, Resolution.

Plan – making preparations for the filming, editing and uploading of a video. This includes strategic as well as practical planning.

Playhead – in a video editing interface, the playhead is the vertical line on the timeline that indicates which part of the timeline you're viewing or working on. When you play the sequence of clips on the timeline, it will play from the position of the playhead. *See also* Timeline.

Presentation – a mode of delivering information through video. It usually consists of a person talking directly into camera. *See also* Delivery mode, Interview, Voice-over.

Presenter – the person appearing in a video speaking directly to the camera.

Publish – to upload content, including video, to a social media channel or website.

Q

Quick-release plate – the detachable plate on the top of a tripod that screws into the base of the mount. *See also* Mount, Tripod.

R

Recce – (pronounced 'reckie') a visit to a location before the shoot to check its potential for filming. During the recce you can assess practicalities such as space, light, noise and accessibility.

Remote server – a computer located somewhere other than your premises on which you store data by purchasing server space. The server is accessed through an internet connection. *See also* Server.

Resolution – in simple terms, resolution refers to the quality of a video image. More specifically it is the number of pixels in an image. If a camera shoots in High Definition, it records images that have 1080 horizontal lines of pixels, with each line containing 1920 pixels. *See also* High definition, Pixel.

Royalty free – a form of music or image licensing. When purchasing royalty free music or images you are buying the license to use the track or image in a specified project, without having to pay the composer or photographer a royalty (a fee) every time it is played.

Rule of framing – how much of a scene the camera operator decides to capture within the video frame. When filming a person, a 'long shot' frames the person from head to foot and a 'close-up' frames only the person's head and shoulders.

Rule of thirds – the concept of the screen being split into thirds horizontally and vertically, with the action or subject being positioned at the intersecting points or along the lines.

S

Script – the information you would like delivered through your video. This can be delivered to camera by a presenter or recorded afterwards as a voice-over. *See also* Presenter, Voice-over.

SD card – a type of memory card onto which data is recorded. There are other types of memory cards, but SD cards are typically used in cameras and mobile devices.

Search terms – a word or combination of words entered into an online search engine to find relevant content. *See also* Keywords.

Search Engine Optimisation (SEO) – the science of increasing the number of visitors to a website by employing various tactics to move the site to a high organic position in search results. *See also* Optimisation.

Security – specifically related to the security of your internet connection. A connection with password protection is more secure than one without, so if you're using a public connection without a password be wary of sending or uploading footage of a confidential or sensitive nature.

Selfie – a photo or video that the camera operator takes of him or herself whilst holding the camera. On a mobile device, you can switch to the front camera for this purpose.

Selfie stick – a mount for a mobile device to enable the recording of selfies more easily.

Sensor – the device in a digital camera that captures the light and converts it to an image. It is the digital version of film.

Sequence – a length of video comprising of individual video clips or shots. *See also* Clip, Shot.

Server – a computer on which data is stored. This could be a local server located on your premises, or a remote server located somewhere else. *See also* Remote server.

Set – a designated area for filming, possibly including a backdrop. If you plan to make multiple videos, you might create a set in an area of your office that can be used again and again.

Shot – a single clip of video. *See also* Clip.

Shooting – the process of filming/capturing footage with a filming device.

Shot list – this is a list of the shots you want to capture for your video. It might include a presentation or an interview as well as supplementary footage. *See also*

Supplementary footage.

Smartphone – a mobile phone that performs many of the functions of a computer; it has a wifi connection and the capability of running applications. *See also* Application, Filming device, Mobile device, Tablet.

Social media – websites and applications that enable multiple users to communicate with one another. Popular social media channels include Facebook, Twitter, Google+ YouTube, Vimeo, Instagram and LinkedIn.

Sound – *see* Audio

Soundbite – a short, spoken statement captured on camera. Testimonial videos are usually made up of short soundbites from happy customers.

Sound meter – a device that provides a visual reading of volume. On a mobile device, a sound meter may look like two vertical or horizontal strips that register different coloured lights as different volume levels are detected. The colours mirror the traffic light system: green for good, orange for danger and red for too loud.

Source footage – unedited video clips, exactly as they were filmed. This is the footage you will use to create a video sequence.

Specifications – a detailed description of the features and functions of a piece of equipment – in this case a mobile device.

Storage capacity – the amount of data a device can hold.

Storage device – the place where you store your footage. It could be an internal hard drive in your tablet or computer, or an external device such as a hard drive, memory card or USB stick.

Subject – the person you are filming. Also referred to as a presenter, interviewee or contributor. *See also* Contributor, Interviewee, Presenter.

Subtitles – a transcription of any dialogue in a video, displayed at the bottom of the video screen as it is spoken. *See also* Closed captions.

Supplementary footage – additional video content that enhances your interview or presentation to help tell the story in a visual way.

T

Tablet – a mobile computer with a touch screen display capable of running applications. *See also* Filming device, Mobile device, Smartphone.

Tags – descriptive keywords added to the video settings of a social media channel to help viewers find your videos.

Take – a filmed version of a particular shot, scene or section of script. *See also* Good take, Outtake

Talking head – this is the phrase used to describe videos that consist of a person talking – either directly into camera, or to an interviewer positioned to one side of the camera. The person in front of the camera is usually framed so just their head and shoulders are visible.

Teaser – a type of video that teases the viewer by holding back certain information. They can be short versions of longer videos, or tasters of an event, product or service.

Text – words positioned on a video screen, placed there during the editing process. It is a way to communicate additional information that the viewer does not learn through dialogue or footage.

Thumbnail image – the 'calling card' of a video; the image used to promote a video,

whether it's on a social media channel, a website or in an email.

Tie-clip microphone – a small microphone that plugs into a mobile device and clips onto the clothing of the person being filmed. *See also* External Microphone.

Tilt – the smooth movement of a camera from up to down (or vice versa) from a fixed position (like nodding your head). *See also* Pan.

Time bar – a counter that runs along the top of the timeline in some video editing programmes, displaying the duration of the edited video sequence. *See also* Timeline.

Timeline – the area of a video editing interface where video clips are assembled into a sequence. *See also* Interface.

Title sequence – the introduction or ending of a video, usually displaying the video's title and other relevant information or contact details.

Tool Palette – the area of a video editing interface containing tools for carrying out editing functions such as trimming, cropping and changing the speed of video clips. *See also* Interface.

Track – a layer in a video editing timeline (video track, audio track) and also a piece of music.

Traffic – the flow of online activity. Website traffic is the data generated by visitors to a website, which shows when they visited, how long they stayed, which pages they visited and their level of engagement on each page.

Trailer – A short version of a longer video that encourages the viewer to watch the longer video, like a film trailer.

Transition – a video editing effect applied between two clips on the timeline to run one clip smoothly into another. Examples of transitions include dissolve, slide, fade and wipe.

TRS/TRRS – A type of jack plug. Newer models of tablet and smartphone tend to take TRRS plugs, while older models take TRS. If you're using an older model of tablet as your filming device with the recommended microphone, you may need a TRS to TRRS adaptor to make it work. *See also* Jack plug.

Tripod – a three-legged stand for supporting a camera or filming device. A video tripod has a head that moves smoothly from side to side or up and down, whereas a photography tripod does not.

U

Uploading – publishing videos to a social media channel, or posting them to a cloud storage solution. Any uploading activity requires an internet connection. *See also* Cloud storage, Publish.

URL – an acronym for Uniform Resource Locator. It is the unique web address for every individual page of online content and can be found in the address bar at the top of the web browser.

V

Video production – the process of making a video from planning, through filming and editing, to uploading.

Video strategy – creating a video strategy simply means setting an objective, identifying your target audience, creating relevant video content then placing it on the channels your target audience uses.

Viewer – the area of a video editing interface where clips can be viewed; a small

video screen. *See also* Interface.

Views – the number of times a video has been viewed by a unique user. Multiple views by the same person don't count, unless they're viewing under a different login.

Vlog – a blog in which the posts are predominantly presented as video.

Vlogger – a person who produces and stars in a video blog, or vlog. *See also* Vlog.

Voice-over – a piece of narration or dialogue in a video not accompanied by footage of the person speaking. *See also* Delivery mode.

W

Web host – the person or company that designs and manages your website. If you made your own website using a template, the host is the template provider.

Wifi – a wireless internet connection. Most mobile devices and modern computers are wifi enabled.

Windows – a computer operating system devised and developed by Microsoft. Other operating systems include iOS (Apple) and Android (Google).

Z

Zoom – a camera function that allows a camera to capture a closer view of something without physically moving closer. Mobile devices use digital zoom instead of specialised zoom lenses, but when digital zoom is employed, the image quality deteriorates the more the camera is zoomed. Instead of using the zoom function, it's advisable to physically move the device closer to the subject.